THE MANUAL OF
PSYCHIC HEALING

YOGI RAMACHARAKA

THE MANUAL OF PSYCHIC HEALING

For information and contact visit our website at:
IndoEuropeanPublishing.com

The present edition is a revised version of 1934 of this work published by the Yogi Publication Society under the title: *The Science of Psychic Healing*, produced in the current edition with completely new, easy to read format, and is set and proofread by Alfred Aghajanian for Indo-European Publishing.

Cover Design by Indo-European Design Team

ISNB: 978-1-60444-040-9

IndoEuropean
Publishing.com
Los Angeles, CA, USA

ORIGINAL PUBLISHER'S NOTICE

This book is not a book of theories—it deals with facts. Its author regards the best of theories as but working hypotheses to be used only until better ones present themselves. The "fact" is the principal thing—the essential thing—to uncover which the tool, theory, is used. The sanest thinkers— the best investigators—hold no theory, not even the one dearest to them, that they are not ready and willing to throw away when a better one presents itself, whether that better one be discovered by themselves or other persons. This is the true philosophical spirit.

It is true that this book may appear dogmatic rather than argumentative. But the author knows of no better way to present the facts of the subject, concisely and to the point—free from the web of theory, and the quicksands of argument. And so he has decided to take the liability of the charge of "dogmatism," in order to deliver his message to you in the style that he feels will reach the greatest number, and thus do the most good.

The facts stated in the book are true, and may be so proven by you in your actual practice, if you will but follow instructions. This, after all, is better than argumentative proofs that fail to prove.

The best way to get the benefit of this book is to start putting its teachings into practice. Do not be content with merely agreeing intellectually to its propositions, but get to work and do something. This is the only way for you to get the benefit of the book—to get your money's worth from the book.

The author has placed in your hands the operation of a mighty force of Nature— you must do the rest. He has pointed out the way—you must take the steps yourself. He has opened the door, but you must walk through it yourself.

We ask the reader to acquaint himself with each and every one of the several methods of healing taught in this book, before he determines which he prefers to use. The wisest will take a little from each, rather than to tie himself down to any particular method or system. All are good, but some will be better for individuals than others. The author mentions this fact, and tells yon how to select.

The methods described in this book may be used in self-healing, even when it is not so stated in the text. In fact, self-healing is probably the favorite idea of the author, who believes in people doing things for themselves, and being independent, so far as is possible.

We trust that you will appreciate the value and simplicity of this book, and will put into practice its important instruction.

THE YOGI PUBLICATION SOCIETY

CONTENTS

CHAPTER I

THE PURPOSE OF THE BOOK

This book is intended to be a plain, simple, practical presentation of the various forms of Psychic Healing. We have said very little about theory—although giving a general outline of the underlying theories that the healer may understand the nature of the work he is doing—and have tried to make the book tell "how" to do the work.

In introducing the subject we wish to say that we have not tried to make a religion of Psychic Healing, for this seems a folly to us. We do not see why Psychic Healing should be made into a religion, any more than should Drug Healing, Massage, Osteopathy, or any other form of healing. All true healing results from an application of perfectly natural laws, and the power employed is as much a natural law as is electricity. For that matter, all

1

natural laws are of "divine" religion, and are equally worthy of respect and reverence.

There has been a great tendency in the Western world to build up religious or semi-religious cults around the work of healing. Each cult or sect claims that its cures and healing is the result of some special creed or metaphysical belief, notwithstanding the fact that the other sects make cures in about the same proportion. The Easterner is not deceived— even self-deceived—in this manner. He is taught from childhood that there are many subtle forces and forms of energy in Nature, which may be taken advantage of and pressed into service by Man. To the Easterner there is as much mystery and awe about electricity as about psychic force—in fact, he sees them as but varying forms of the same thing, and he respects them both. A little reflection will teach anyone that this is correct. All Energy and Force is a manifestation of Prana (the Hindu term for the Principle of Energy) and the Easterner teachings are that Prana has Mind behind it—that it emerged from the Mind Principle of the Universe. We cannot speak at length of these theories here, and must refer students to our "Advanced Course in Yogi Philosophy" for fuller information, if they desire the same.

The above facts being true, it follows that the Eastern psychic healer fails to feel that jealousy and prejudice regarding practitioners of other forms of healing, which, alas, is so prevalent in the Western world. He believes that any form of true healing employs the same force and power that he is using notwithstanding the difference in the methods and he respects the same accordingly. He naturally prefers his own method, but does not abuse his neighbor for preferring another method.

Moreover, the Easterner healer is taught from the beginning that there are certain natural laws of the body, which must be observed in order to maintain health, or to restore it if lost. He believes that that which makes the healthy man healthy will make the sick man well. We allude to the natural laws regarding nutrition, elimination, breathing, etc. We have set forth our conception of these laws in our book, "Hatha Yoga," and will briefly mention the same in the succeeding chapter entitled "The Natural Laws of the Body, to which we refer all students, strongly advising them to acquaint themselves with these natural laws before attempting healing work. We are fully aware that many Western schools of Psychic Healing ignore these laws as too "material", but one has but to look around him to see the folly of that position. Natural laws may not be defied with impunity.

We believe that if people would follow the teachings of "Hatha Yoga" there would be no need for healing of any sort, for all would maintain health. But people will not do this, and therefore healing methods are necessary. And we believe that Psychic Healing is the best and highest form of Healing known to man. But even Psychic Healing will not, and cannot, effect a *permanent* cure, unless the patient will change his or her habits of living, and will endeavor to live in accordance with Nature's laws.

So therefore, again and again, do we urge the healer to acquaint his patient with these natural laws of the body — "Hatha Yoga" — and while giving the healing treatments he should endeavor to "work in" advice and instruction regarding the natural laws of the body, so that when the patient is healed he will live in such a manner as to promote health, and to hold the ground he has gained, and not slip back again.

We believe that these two books — companion books "Hatha Yoga" and "Psychic Healing" will give one the "Key to Health."

This book is not intended as a treatise upon disease. On the contrary, it says as little as possible about disease, and prefers to keep before the eye of the student the Healthy Condition, and the means of bringing it about. Therefore you will see but little of symptoms in this book. Symptoms are but various indications of a cause behind them, and we believe that there is only one general cause for disease, and that is improper functioning of the cells. In other words, we believe that all disease is but Cell-disease. And we believe that the general treatments given in connection with the principles laid down in "Hatha Toga," will remove the cause of the trouble, and the symptoms will then disappear.

We will not take up your attention with praise of the systems of healing taught in this book. We believe that "the proof of the pudding lies in the eating," and we say to you, "Try It."

Have confidence in yourself, and in your healing power. It is your Divine heritage, and is not a gift bestowed upon but a few. It is a general gift and natural power that may be developed by practice and confidence, and instead of decreasing by use, it grows in proportion to its use. It is like a muscle that is developed by practice, but which becomes soft and flabby by non-use.

But when you begin to make cures, and hear wonderful reports of your success, which may seem miraculous to those around you who do not understand the subject, do not become puffed up or conceited, and begin to believe that you have some special gift or power. This is folly, for all healers are but channels of expression through which the natural forces and energies flow. You are but an instrument in the hands of Natural Laws. Do not forget this. This thought may be turned into a source of strength if you will look at the other side of the proposition and remember that *you have the forces of the Universe back of you.*

We advise the student to carefully study, and acquaint himself with all of the methods taught in this book. After doing so, let him select the methods that appeal most to him—being guided by his intuition. Let him, if he is so led, take a little from one system and a little from another, and combine them into a system of his own. Let him "take his own wherever he finds it". Do not deem it necessary, to tie yourself to any one system, to wear the "label" or "tag" of any one school. Beware of labels and tags on the mind. Be YOUR SELF.

CHAPTER II

NATURAL LAWS OF THE BODY

As we have stated in our last chapter, we believe that the true secret of Health lies in the observance of the Natural Laws of the Body. These Laws may be summed up as Right Living and Right Thinking. In our book, "Hatha Yoga," we have explained our conceptions of these laws at considerable length and detail. We do not hesitate to state positively that every healer, or searcher for health, should acquaint himself with the instructions given in that book. Without an understanding of these fundamental laws any and all forms of healing are but temporary makeshifts, and the patient, if he pursues the former improper modes of Living and Thinking, will relapse into his old condition when the treatments are discontinued. There can be no successful defiance of Natural Laws.

In this chapter we will run briefly over the principal

laws described in "Hatha Yoga" for the benefit of those readers who have not acquainted themselves with the contents of that book. But this chapter cannot begin to give the "Hatha Toga" instruction fully for that fills a good-sized book of itself.

In the first place, there can be no Health without proper nutrition. And there can be no proper nutrition without proper assimilation. This being granted, it may be seen that one of the first things for a healer to do is to re-establish normal conditions in this respect, and build up proper assimilation. This is why we have urged the healer to begin all treatments—for all kinds of complaints—with a treatment of the stomach, to restore normal conditions there. The stomach should be treated first, last and always, for there lies the secret of the first step toward recovery. In fact, the majority of diseases may be traced directly to the stomach, and to imperfect nutrition and assimilation. A man can no more thrive on non-nutritious food, or food imperfectly assimilated, than can a tree or plant or animal. Imperfect nutrition causes the blood to become poor and weak, and consequently every cell in the body becomes weakened and starved, and even the brain cells suffer with the rest, and are unable to send the proper currents of vital force and energy to the other parts of the body.

Always begin treatments by treating the stomach

thoroughly, by whatever method you use. Insist that it take care of the food given it, and that it assimilates the food and converts it into good rich nourishing blood, which will flow to all parts of the body, giving health and strength. And insist upon your patient partaking of nourishing food in sufficient quantities.

One of the best ways to get the full nourishment of the food partaken of is by perfect Mastication. Food perfectly masticated gives the full amount of nourishment contained within it, which food, half - chewed and "bolted," wastes the greater part of its nourishment. We urge the importance of this matter upon the healer. We have seen cases of ill-nourished people restored to health in a very short time, merely from the change in the manner of masticating the food. All food should be chewed until it becomes soft, pulpy and pasty.

The second important point is the Irrigation of the body, as we have called it in "Hatha Yoga" we mean the proper use of Water. The physical system requires a certain amount of fluids daily, in order to do its work properly. About two quarts of fluid in twenty four hours is the normal amount for an adult. Without the proper amount of water the body is unable to do its work properly and the system suffers. Perfect secretion and excretion requires the normal amount of fluids. Otherwise the secreting glands are unable to manufacture the juices and fluids needed in digestion, absorption and assimilation, and the excreting glands are unable to provide for the excretion or throwing out of the waste products of the system through the kidneys and bowels. The liver is unable to act without sufficient fluids, and the other organs likewise suffer.

The third requisite for health is correct breathing. "When you realize that unless correct breathing is performed by the patient the blood is imperfectly oxygenated, and is therefore unable to perform its functions, yon will begin to see why a person breathing improperly is unable to have health. Practice deep breathing yourself until you understand it perfectly and then instruct your patient in the art. Our little book, "The Science of Breath," gives full and complete direction for correct "breathing. We advise you to acquaint yourself with its contents.

Exercise, Bathing, etc., are important things to be observed. The healer should inform the patient as to this fact. Sleep is a needed something that Nature insists upon. Without a sufficient degree of rest the brain becomes over-worked and complications set in.

In short, the patient should be instructed to become

a normal, sane, natural being. Stick as closely as possible to Nature, and she will do the rest. The Natural Laws are designed for the furtherance of Health, and if not interfered with will produce and maintain normal conditions. The trouble with us is that modern "civilization" has drawn us so far away from Nature, that our natural impulses and tendencies have been smothered and stifled, and we have ceased to listen to Nature's voice until she has become disheartened and has ceased to call us. The only sane plan is to get back to Nature as near to her as possible. Live as natural a life as possible and you will have the reward that Nature bestows upon those who are true to her.

Our book, "Hatha Yoga" is the Yogi conception of the natural life. Natural life is taught on every page. It holds that there is a great Intelligence permeating all Life, and that every natural law is a Divine Law, and should be so regarded and observed.

We urge upon every healer the duty and privilege that is his to educate and inform the patients to whose aid he is called in these laws of Right Living and Right Thinking. This particular book is not designed to repeat the instruction contained in "Hatha Yoga," but instead is designed to supplement it to the end that those who have violated Nature's Laws and who are suffering therefrom may be speedily brought back to normal conditions the condition of Health and again started on the road of Life.

The healer should be more than a healer. He should be an instructor and educator of the people. In this way he makes his calling a divine and sacred one, instead of that of a mere tinkerer of bodies. Keep this ideal ever before you, and your work will be one of the greatest pleasure as well as of the greatest success. Remember the Brotherhood of Man, and realize that your work in the world is to spread the glad tidings of Health and Strength, and lead your brothers back to Mother Nature, from whose bosom they have strayed.

CHAPTER III

THE INSTINCTIVE MIND

In our "Fourteen Lessons" we called your attention to the various Planes of the Mind, and, among others, the Instinctive Mind. This plane of the Mind, as we told you, controls and manages the growth, nourishment and operation of the physical body— every operation and function of every organ, part and cell being under the control and direction of thin part of the mind. This part of the mind never sleeps, but attends to its duties while the Reasoning faculties are quieted in slumber and rest.

The constant work of repair, replacement, change, digestion, assimilation, elimination, etc., is performed by this part of the mind, all below the plane of consciousness. The wondrous work of the body is carried on on this plane of mind, without our conscious knowledge. The intelligent work of the cells, cell-groups, ganglia, organ intelligences, etc., are under the superintendence of this plane of mind.

In our next chapter we give you a short account of this wonderful world of cell life that exists in every human organism. We advise you to read that chapter, as it will throw light on many puzzling questions, and will enable you to direct your healing powers intelligently.

The Instinctive Mind is not confined to the brain as a seat of operations, but is distributed over the entire nervous system, the spinal column and solar plexus being important centers for its operations.

One of the most important facts that we have to consider in connection with the Instinctive Mind, in this book, is that it is susceptible of interference on the part of the Conscious Mind. This interference may be for good or bad, according to the nature of the "suggestions" passed on by the Conscious Mind.

In our chapter on Suggestion we have given a number of instances to illustrate the effect of the mind on the bodily functions. This effect of thought is occasioned by the Conscious Mind passing on suggestions to the Instinctive Mind, which then proceeds to act upon them. Many a man has become sick by reason of adverse and hurtful suggestions accepted by him and passed on to his Instinctive

Mind. In the same way a sick man has been restored to health, by positive and helpful suggestions accepted and passed on in the same manner. And in both cases, remember, the diseased condition and the restored healthy condition were occasioned by perfectly natural process, by the Instinctive Mind passing on its orders to its subordinate parts, cells, organs, etc.

We do not think it worth while to enter into a long discussion of the various theories advanced to account for the existence and operation of the Instinctive Mind. This book is intended to tell you "how" to make cures, and all the theory we think it worth while to give you is a mere general outline for the purpose of an intelligent comprehension of the process of the cure. To wander off into an extended discussion of the theories regarding mind, or the speculations regarding life and what lies back of life, would be out of place. We believe in keeping each subject to itself, believing that in this way the student is better able to concentrate upon the particular subject under consideration. The workings of the Instinctive Mind will appear as you proceed with the study of the methods of treatment. The next chapter which deals with Cell life, will also throw further light on the subject.

CHAPTER IV

MIND IN CELLS, AND CELL COMMUNITIES

In order to understand the nature of Psychic Healing one must have an acquaintance with the nature of the mental side of the Body. Not only has the Central Mind a number of Planes of Manifestation, but each organ has something which might be called an organic mind, made up of a "group-mind" of a number of cells, each of which cells moreover has a cell-mind of its own. This idea is somewhat startling to those who have not acquainted themselves with the details of the subject, but it is known to be correct, not only by the Yogis, but also by those who have familiarized themselves with the recent discoveries of Western Science. Let us take a hasty look at this cell-life.

As we told you in the "Fourteen Lessons", the Yogi Philosophy teaches that the physical body is built up of "little lives" or cell lives, and that each cell had an independent action, in addition to a cell-community action. These little "lives" are really minds of a certain degree of development, sufficient to enable them to do their work properly. These bits of mind are, of course, subordinate to the control of the Instinctive Mind of the individual, and will readily obey orders from that source, as well as from the Intellect.

These cell minds manifest a peculiar adaptation for their particular work. Their selective action in extracting from the blood the nourishment needed, and rejecting that which is not needed, is an instance of this intelligence. The process of digestion, assimilation, etc., shows the "mind" of the cell, either individual or in groups. The healing of wounds the rush of the cells to the point where they are required, and many other instances familiar to physiologists are evidence of this cell life and mental action.

The entire body is built up of these tiny cells. This is true not only of the soft tissue and muscle, but also of the hard bony parts, including the enamel of the teeth. These cells are shaped in accordance with the particular work that they are designed to perform, such shapes and forms varying materially. Each cell is, practically, an individual, separate and more or less independent, although subject to the control of the organic mind, and, still higher, the Instinctive Mind.

The cells are constantly at work—each performing his own particular task, like a well trained soldier in an army. Some of the cells are active workers, and others are of the reserve force, kept awaiting some sudden and urgent call to duty. Some are stationery, and others are moving about attending to their particular duties and tasks. Some of them act as the scavengers of the system, carrying away the refuse and debris of the system, while others carry the nourishing elements of the food to all parts of the body.

Cell life has been compared to a large and well ordered community, each individual doing his own particular work all—for the common good. The community is a large one, it being estimated that there are at least 75,000,000,000 of the red blood cells alone. These red blood cells are the common carriers of the body, and float in the arteries and veins, carrying a load of oxygen from the lungs and delivering particles of it to the various tissues of the body, which give life and strength to the particular parts. On their return journey through the veins the cells carry with them the waste products of the system. Like a merchant vessel, these cells carry a cargo on their outgoing trip, and bring back a second cargo on their return. Other cells perform police work and protect the system from bacteria, etc., which might produce trouble in the system. These policemen are quite savage, and usually get rid of the intruder by devouring him, but if unable to so dispose of him they rally in number and finally eject him from the system in the shape of a boil, pimple, etc.

The cells enable the body to carry on its work of continual regeneration. Every part of our bodies are being repaired constantly by fresh material. And the cells do the work. Millions of these little workers are constantly moving along, or else working in a fixed position in the parts of our bodies, renewing the worn-out tissues and replacing them with new material, and at the same time throwing out of the system the worn-out and discarded material.

Each of the cells of the body, no matter how humble may be its functions, is possessed of an Instinctive knowledge of that which is vital to its life-work, and its own life. It takes nourishment, and reproduces itself by increasing in size and then separating. It seems to have a memory, and in other ways manifests mind action. We do not consider it necessary to go deeply into this matter at this point, and merely mention these facts that the reader may understand that these cells are "living things," having mind action.

These cells are built up into organs, parts, tissue, muscle, etc., and form what is known as cell-communities, in which their minds seem to combine, in addition to their having independent mental action. In the case of the liver, for instance, the millions of cells composing that organ have a community-mind, which may be called the "liver-mind," and which acts as an "entity" subject, always, to the control of the Instinctive Mind. This is a most important fact to remember, in connection with psychic healing, for the whole principle of the latter depends upon the fact that these organs, through their minds, are amenable to Mental Control and Direction.

As we have said, each cell belongs to a cell- group; and each group forms a part of a larger group, and so on until the whole forms a great group or whole community of cells, under the control of the Instinctive Mind. And the little minds of the entire cell community combine under the control of that great Instinctive Mind. And, at the same time, there are lesser combinations, and still lesser, until the mind of the single cell is reached. The entire mental organism of the cells is something quite wonderful, and startling.

The control of these cell-communities is one of the

duties of the Instinctive Mind, and it usually does its work very well, unless interfered with by the Intellect, which sometimes sends it fear-thoughts and demoralizes it. The Intellect insists upon interfering with the established order of the body, and by introducing strange customs and habits, tends to demoralize the cell-communities and to bring disorder into their ranks.

Sometimes something akin to rebellion springs up among these cell-communities or groups, and they revolt at working overtime, or from similar reasons. In this connection we take the liberty of quoting from our book entitled "Hatha Yoga," which gives a clear idea of these cell rebellions. The book says: "At times it seems that some of the smaller groups (and even some of the larger on certain occasions) go on a strike, rebelling against unaccustomed and improper work forced upon them working overtime and similar causes, such as a lack of proper nourishment. These little cells often act just as would men under the same circumstances—the analogy is often startling to the observer and investigator. These rebellions or strikes seem to spread, if matters are not arranged, and even when matters are patched up, the cells seem to return to their work in a sullen manner, and, instead of doing their work the best they know how, they will do as little as possible, and only just when they feel like it. A restoration of normal conditions, resulting from improved nutrition, proper attention, etc., will gradually bring about a return to normal functioning, and matters may be very much expedited by orders from the Will, directed immediately to the cell-groups. It is astonishing how soon order and discipline may be restored in this way."

Science has shown us the truth of the old Yogi teachings that all disease was cell-disease, and it follows that if we can manage to get control of the cell-trouble, we have mastered the entire problem. This control may be acquired in a number of ways, and the explanation of these ways and their method of application, forms the subject of this book.

CHAPTER V

THE THREE FORMS OF PSYCHIC HEALING

As we stated at the close of our last chapter, the control of the cells manifesting physical disease, might be accomplished by the several forms of Psychic Healing, which may be considered in three forms known as :

(1) Pranic Healing, or healing by the sending of Prana or Vital Force to the affected parts, thereby stimulating the cells and tissue to normal activity, the result being that the waste matter is ejected from the system, and normal conditions restored. This form of healing is known in the Western world as "Magnetic Healing," etc., and many cures have been made by reason thereof, although many of the healers have not known the principles underlying the work, although they had acquired very good working knowledge of the methods to be employed.

(2) Mental Healing, by which is meant the control of the cell-minds, either direct, or through the Instinctive Mind of the sick person. This form of Healing includes what is known in the Western World as Mental Healing, direct and absent; Suggestive Healing; Psychic Healing, etc., etc., etc., and includes many so-called religious forms of healing which are but forms of Mental Healing, disguised under the cover of religious teachings and theories.

(3) Spiritual Healing, by which is meant a high form of healing arising from the Healer possessing a high degree of Spiritual Unfoldment, and allowing the light of his or her, higher mentality to pour forth upon the mind of the patient, bathing him in a wave of high thought and lifting him, temporarily to a higher plane of being. This form of healing is not nearly so common as one might be led to believe from listening to the talk of the healers and their patients. In fact it is very rare, and none but healers of a very high order possess it. Many who think that they have it, are simply using the ordinary methods of Mental Healing, and have not the slightest idea of what true Spiritual Healing consists. But, no harm is done, so long as the results are obtained, and we merely mention the matter here, that the reader may form a clear idea of the entire subject. Each of these forms of Psychic Healing will be considered in turn,

as we proceed.

The principal point to be remembered, at this point is that at the last all forms of Psychic Healing are forms of Mental Healing. Even the healing by Prana, is Mental Healing, for the Prana is moved by the Mind, and in fact, is the power of Mind itself, as we shall see presently. The disease or trouble is called "physical," that is, is manifest in the cells of the physical body, and, if we examine it closely we will see that it is really a mental trouble of the particular cells affected. And, consequently the only way a cure may be affected, is by reaching the mental part of the cell, and rousing it to normal activity. This may be accomplished in many ways, but all ways, at the last are Mental Ways, for it is not the "way" that works the cure, but the mind that is aroused by the Way. These points will be brought out as we proceed.

In our next chapter, we shall consider the form of Psychic Healing called Pranic Healing.

CHAPTER VI

THE PRINCIPLES OF PRANIC HEALING

Before we can understand Pranic Healing, we must understand something about Prana. Prana is the name given by the Yogi philosophers to "Vital Force," or Energy, which is found within the body of every living thing. It may be called the Life Force. At the last, Prana is known to be Mental in its nature, and is the Energy of the Mind of the Universe. But in order to avoid metaphysical distinctions in this book, let us follow the usual custom of treating Prana as an independent thing, just as we do Mind and Matter.

The Yogis teach that Prana is a Universal Principle—a something pervading all Space, and together with Mind and Matter composing the Threefold Manifestation of the Absolute. Leaving aside the manifestations of Prana in the forms of

26

Force, known as Electricity, Heat, Light, etc., let us consider it in its manifestation of Vital Force, which is the only aspect with which we are concerned in this book. Prana is the Force by which all activity is carried on in the body—by which all bodily movements are possible—by which all functioning is done—by which all signs of life manifest themselves. We have described Prana at considerable length in our other books, and do not desire to repeat ourselves, and to take up space in such repetitions, any more than can be avoided.

Briefly, however, we may say that Prana is that Principle of Life which is found in the air, water, food, etc., from which the living organism absorbs it to use in the work of the body. We advise all students of this book to read either the "Science of Breath" or else "Hatha Yoga" in order to gain a fuller idea of the subject of Prana. In the books named, we have given many exercises whereby Prana may be stored up and acquired, and also how it may be used.

The general principles of Pranic Healing rests on the fact that Prana may be transferred or transmitted from one person to another, in many ways. The usual method, and the most effective is to use the hands and make passes over the sick person, and at the same time directing a current of Prana to the affected part, thereby stimulating and stirring into

27

activity the sluggish cell-groups. The Prana so transferred acts as a bracing tonic to the patient, and invigorates and strengthens him wonderfully, besides tending to produce the local improvement, just noted.

Prana may also be sent to the patient in the shape of Energized Thought, directed from the Mind of the Healer. This fact has not generally been brought out in works on the subject, but we shall pay much attention to it in our consideration of Pranic Healing, in our next chapter. In fact, very wonderful healing work may be performed by those methods alone, without reference to the other phases of Healing.

The student will notice that we are not carry on long to discuss theories. This is done purposely, for we wish to make this book a book of practical facts, and instruction, and the majority of the theories will be familiar to those who have read our other books, which, although not devoted to the subject of healing, nevertheless, touch upon the general theories underlying all psychic phenomena.

Healing of the sick by means of "laying on of hands" has been known from the earliest days of the human race. As far back in history as we are able to go, we may find trace of this practice. And, it is only fair to surmise that before the days of written history, the custom was likewise prevalent. It is found among all races of people today, even among the "primitive" races. It seems to have arisen from an instinctive conviction in he mind of man, that healing lay in that direction.

The Indians, the Egyptians, the Jews, the Chinese, of ancient days, were perfectly familiar with this form of healing. In Egypt the ancient carvings in the rocks show healers treating patients by placing one hand on the stomach, and the other on the back. And the early explorers of China report that similar practices were common there.

The Old Testament is full of instances of this form of healing. And we also find cases mentioned in the New Testament. St. Patrick is reported to have healed the blind in Ireland, by placing his hands upon their eyes. St. Bernard is reported as having cured eleven blind people, and to have enabled eighteen lame persons to regain the use of the limbs, all in one day; and in Cologne he is reported to have cured twelve lame people, also three dumb persons, and ten deaf ones, all by means of the laying on of hands. The history of the early church is full of instances of this sort, and making allowance for the romantic tales that always arise in such cases, we may see that much good and effective work was done by these people, in this way.

Pyrrhus, the king of Epirus, is reported by history to

have had the power of curing colic and diseases of the spleen, by touching the persons affected. The Emperor Vespasian is said to have cured nervous diseases, and lameness, blindness, etc., by laying on of hands. Hadrian cured people having dropsical diseases, by applying the points of his fingers to them. King Olaf healed instantaneously by laying his hands upon the sufferer. The early kings of England and France healed bronchocele and throat affections by the "King's touch." In England there was a disease called "the King's evil," which was thought to be curable only by the touch of the King.

The Courts of Hapsburg were believed to be able to cure stammering by a kiss. Pliny reports that in the ancient days there were men who cured the bites of serpents by the touch. Numerous religious celebrities cured disease by the laying on of hands. In England, Greatrakes created quite a sensation, and invited persecution, by going about curing all sorts of diseases in this way—his success in curing diseases that had been thought to be curable by the "King's touch" caused many to regard him as a pretender to the throne. In the seventeenth century a gardener named Levret performed wonderful cures in the streets of London, by stroking the afflicted with his fingers. In 1817, a Sicilian in-keeper named Eichter cured thousands of people by applying his hands to them.

So you see, the fact of Pranic Healing has made itself apparent in all ages and among all people, and those having sufficient confidence in themselves to perform cures, were looked upon as specially gifted persons. But the fact is that the "gift" is one common to the human race, and may be manifested by anyone who has sufficient confidence in himself to try it, and who has sufficient earnestness to "throw his heart" into the work.

The old Yogi teachers of over twenty five centuries ago, had reduced this form of healing to a science, and traces of their knowledge filtered out to all parts of the world. The Egyptians obtained their knowledge from the great Yogi teachers, and established schools of their own. The Greeks obtained a similar knowledge from India and Egypt. And the Hebrews and Assyrians are believed to have obtained theirs through Egyptian channels. The early Greek physicians performed their principal cures by the laying on of hands, and manipulation of the affected parts of the body. With them the healing process was something belonging to the orders of the priesthood, and the general public were not allowed to participate in its mysteries. Hippocrates has written: "The affections suffered by the body, the soul sees quite well with. shut eyes. Wise physicians, even among the ancients, were aware how beneficial to the blood is to make slight frictions with the hands over the body. It is believed by many experienced doctors that the heat which oozes out of the hand, on being applied to the sick, is highly salutary and nourishing. The remedy has been, found to be applicable to sudden as well as habitual pains, and various species of debility, being both renovating and strengthening in its effects. It has often appeared, while I have thus been soothing my patients, as if there were a singular property in my hands to pull and draw away from the affected parts aches and diverse impurities by laying my hand on the place, and by extending my fingers toward it. Thus it is known to some of the learned that health may be implanted in the sick by certain gestures, and by contact, as some diseases may be communicated from one to another."

Aesculapius treated diseases by breathing on the affected parts, and by stroking them with his hands. The ancient Druids, that is the priesthood, performed cures in this way, the same being made a part of their religious ceremonies and rites. Tacitus, Vopiscus, and Lampridius, report these things of the Druids, and give wonderful testimony regarding their "gifts".

The records of the Middle Ages are filled with similar accounts of wonderful cures accomplished by the laying on of the hands, the churches being the usual scene of the cures. Van Helmont, who lived about the first part of the seventeenth century, seemed to be acquainted with the principles of Pranic healing, for he writes: "Magnetism is active everywhere, and there is nothing new in it but the name; it is a paradox only to those who ridicule everything, and who attribute to the power of Satan whatever they are unable to explain."

About the same time, a Scotchman named Maxwell, taught similar methods of healing. He believed in a vital spirit pervading the universe, which man could draw upon in order to cure diseases. In 1734, Father Hehl, a priest, taught the existence of an "universal fluid," which might be used to cure diseases. He made many wonderful cures, but was driven out of the church for possessing the power of the devil, and using witchcraft. Mesmer taught the theory of Animal Magnetism, and accomplished cures by its aid, always using his hands in applying it Mesmer left many followers and disciples, many of whom gained great prominence, the Marquis of Puysegur being one of these.

In Germany Mesmer's doctrines, and those that grew of them, gained great popularity and prominence. Bremen was a great centre of the "Animal Magnetism" doctrine, and from there it spread all over Germany. The Prussian government took a great interest in the matter, and established a hospital for the cure of diseases by "magnetic" treatment. Various Continental governments passed rigid laws keeping the magnetic treatments in the hands of the medical fraternity.

And, so from country to country, the new doctrines spread Often repressed by governmental interference, urged on by medical opposition, it still flourishes in various forms, and under different theories. During the past several years it has gained great prominence in America and Great Britain, both from the various schools of "Magnetic Healing," as well as from the tremendous growth of the "New Thought movement." Many theories have been evolved to account for it, ranging from purely material ones to religious conceptions. But, not withstanding the theories, the work went on, and cures were accomplished. The laying on of hands played a prominent part in nearly all these forms of healings, in spite of their theories or names of their schools.

Many people still believe that this form of healing is some sort of special gift, inherent in, and bestowed upon certain individuals. But this is not so, for the "gift" of healing is inherent in each person, although some attain more proficiency than others, by reason of their peculiar temperamental adaptability for the work. And all may cultivate and develop this "gift."

We do not care to devote a great deal of space to the

theory underlying Pranic Healing—for all the various forms of healing by the laying on of hands, really comes under this head, in spite of conflicting theories and names. But we may as well briefly run over the fundamental ideas underlying the subject.

Perhaps the better way would be to identify the word "Prana," with that which we recognize as Vital Force, so we will use the word Vital Force, in this chapter, in our work of explaining the nature of Prana.

Vital Force is that which underlies all physical action of the body. It is that which causes the circulation of the blood—the movements of the cells—in fact all the motions upon which depend the life of the physical body. Without this Vital Force, there could be no life—no motion—no action. Some call it "nervous force," but it is the one thing, no matter by what name it may be called. It is this force that is sent forth from the nervous system by an effort of the will, when we wish a muscle to move. And it is this force which causes that muscle to move.

It is not necessary to go into a discussion of the real nature and essence of this Vital Force, for that would carry us far into other phases of the subject. Enough for our purpose is the fact that it really exists, and may be used in the healing of disease. The electrician—even the most advanced men of that science—know nothing of the real nature of Electricity, and yet they are able to make wonderful use of it, and to understand its laws of operation. And so it is with this matter of Vital Force, for to understand its real nature and origin, one would need to know the real nature and origin of the Universe. But, man may, and does, use this force every moment of his life, and may turn it to account in other ways, such as the healing of the sick.

Man absorbs his supply of Vital Force from the food he eats; the water he drinks; and largely from the air he breathes. He also has a mental source of energy, whereby he draws to himself energy from the great reservoirs of Energy, of the Universal Mind. In our books "Science of Breath" and "Hatha Yoga," we have gone into this matter at greater length, and all students of Psychic Healing should acquaint themselves with those books, if they have not done so already. This Vital Energy is stored up in the Brain, and great nerve centers of the body, from which it is drawn to supply the constantly arising wants of the system. It is distributed over the wires of the nervous system, to all parts of the body. In fact, every nerve is constantly charged with Vital Force, which is replenished when exhausted. Every nerve is a "live wire" through which the flow of Vital Force proceeds. And, more than this, every cell in the body, no matter where it is located, or what work it is doing, contains more or less Vital Energy, at all times.

A strong healthy person, is one who is charged with a goodly supply of Vital Force, which travels to all parts of the body, refreshing, stimulating, and producing activity and energy. Not only does it do this, but it surrounds his body like an aura, and may be felt by those coming in contact. A person depleted of Vital Force will manifest ill-health, lack of vitality, etc., and will only regain his normal condition when he replenishes his store of Vitality.

While the medical fraternity are quite free to express their belief in the existence of Vital Force although they differ in their theories regarding the nature of the same they insist that it cannot be transferred beyond the limits of the nervous system of the person producing or manifesting it. But this is contradicted by the actual experiences of thousands of people who know that Vital Force, Prana, or Magnetism, call it what you will, may be, and has been transmitted to the body of a third person, who is thereby strengthened and invigorated by reason thereof.

Many of the advocates and practitioners of this form of Healing have caused a confusion in the public mind by calling it "Magnetism," or "Magnetic Healing etc. There is nothing "Magnetic" about this Vital Force, for it arises from an entirely different cause, although, to be sure, all forms of Force or Energy arise from the same primal cause. Vital Force is something which plays its own part in the economy of Nature, and that part is entirely different from that played by Magnetism. It is something different from anything else, and can be compared only with itself.

All persons have more or less Vital Force, and all persons have the power of increasing their store, and of transmitting it to others, and thereby curing disease. In other words all persons are potential healers. There has been much talk about persons being "gifted" in this form of Healing, but the fact is that all persons have the "gift," and may develop it by confidence and practice. And this development is the purpose of this part of the book.

The principles of Pranic Healing is the filling of the cells of the affected part with a fresh and full supply of Vital Force or Prana, whereby the cells are enabled to regain normal powers of functioning, and work, the consequence being that when the cells work properly, the organ recovers its former activity, and the entire system regains Health and Health, after all, is merely Normal Functioning.

CHAPTER VII

THE PRACTICE OF PRANIC HEALING

The use of the hands in healing seems to be the result of an instinctive tendency of the human race. The mother naturally places her hands on the head of the child who runs to her with a story of a fall, or hurt, and the child seems to be quieted and relieved by the application of the mother's hands. How many times do we see and hear mothers relieving their children in this way, saying: "Now, dear, it is all right Mother has made it all right now run away and play." And the child departs, its tears drying on its cheeks.

Or, if any of us hurt ourselves, how natural it is to place the hands on the part, and getting relief in that way. The curing of headaches by the application of the hands, is quite common, and the touch of the hand of the nurse brings relief to the sick person.

39

And these simple movements—almost instinctive in their nature—from the basis of the practice of Pranic Healing. The process is so simple, that it scarcely needs to be taught, although in this book we shall present to your attention some of the best methods practiced by those who have attained proficiency in the science of this form of healing.

The principal means of conveying Vital Force or Prana, in healing, are known as (1) Gazing, or transmitting by the eye; (2) Passes, or transmitting by the hands; and (3) Breathing, or transmitting by the breath. All of these methods are efficacious, and, in fact, all may be used conjointly with the others.

Inasmuch as the transmission of the Vital Force is largely Mental, and as the eye is a well known channel of conveying Mental Force, it follows that the eye may be advantageously used in conveying or transmitting Vital Force in healing. In the process of healing, when passes are being made over the affected part, the healer will find that it will increase the effect if he will look intently at the part being treated, and in so doing concentrate his mind, and "will" that Power be transferred to the part, and the diseased cells be given strength to properly perform their work.

Many healers use the breath, during healing, with excellent results. It is usually applied by breathing directly upon the affected parts, in which the warm breath seems to have a wonderfully stimulating effect. It is also applied by breathing on a piece of flannel fabric applied directly over the affected part, in which the fabric retains much of the heat, and soon grows too warm for comfort. These forms will be noted as we proceed.

But the principal means of transmitting the Vital Force, in this form of Healing, is by the use of the hands, by means of Passes and Manipulations. We shall consider the process of making Passes, first, and will then take up the several forms of manipulation.

The position of the hands in making the Passes may be described as follows:

Hold the hands well apart, with the fingers extended and separated. If your patient be seated, raise your hand above his head, and then bring them down before him, slowly and gradually, until you finish with a sweeping motion about the knees. When the pass is completed, swing the fingers sideways, as if you were throwing water from them, and then bring up the hands *with fingers closed*, forming the upward movement, along the sides of the patient, with the palms of the hands toward his sides. Then, when the hands reach over his head, again bring them down in front of him, with the fingers extended. By keeping the idea that you are bathing him in a flow of Vital Force, which is pouring from your finger ends, you will soon acquire the power motion, and, after all, each healer has his own favorite motions, which come to him instinctively. The downward motions of the hands, bring a restful feeling to the patient, while an upward movement in front of the face causes a feeling of wakefulness, and activity.

There are a number of variations in the several passes, etc., which we shall now consider. The student is advised to acquaint himself with the various movements, that he may not appear awkward when he practices on some person desiring relief. Familiarity with the movements imparts a confidence that cannot be acquired otherwise, and besides, it leaves the mind of the healer free from bother about details, and enables him to concentrate his attention on the work of healing.

Longitudinal Passes are passes made in a downward direction along the body, such as we have mentioned above. They are made along the part affected, whether that part be the head, chest, limbs, or any special part of the body. They are always made downward, and never upward. As we have said above, the idea to be kept in the mind is that you are pouring out a stream of Vital Force from the tips of your fingers. Your fingers must be spread out (as above stated) and the palm must be underneath. The movements must be down, with fingers extended, but the upward movements must be made along the sides of the patient, with fingers closed, and palms turned toward the sides of the patient. No special distance is to be observed, this matter being left to your instinctive sense, which will soon inform you as to the right distance, which will be found to be much nearer in some cases than in others. When you feel that the distance is "just about right," then be satisfied that you have caught the proper distance at which the best effects may be produced.

In a general way, however, it may be said that a slow movement, at a distance of say three or four inches from the body, produces a sense of comfort, rest, and relief. A rather more rapid movement made at the distance of say one foot, seems to have a more stimulating effect, and causes a sense of activity and energy in the parts. A still more stimulating effect is obtained, when the passes are made more rapidly and vigorously, at a distance of say two feet from the body. These last mentioned passes, tend to stimulate the circulation, and to arouse activity in sluggish organs.

Transversal Passes are passes made across the body or part. They are made by turning the hands so that the palms will be sideways and outward, instead of inward. This will require a peculiar turning of the wrist, but the position will soon become easy. When the hands are in the right position, sweep them out, sideways, before the body or part, and in bringing them back, reverse the palms so that they are inward, and facing each other, instead of having their backs to each other. These passes have been found to be very efficacious in "loosening up" the affected parts, where congestion has occurred. It is often well to give this form of treatment, before giving the regular Longitudinal Passes.

A valuable form of treatment, in some cases, is what is known as Palmar Presentation. This is accomplished by presenting the palm of the hand to the affected part, at a distance of about six inches, or even a little nearer, and holding it there for several minutes. This is usually performed with one hand alone. It has a stimulating and strengthening effect.

Akin to this is what is known as Digital Presentation, which consists in extending and presenting the fingers of the right hand toward the affected part, at a distance of six inches, and holding them there for several minutes, allowing the Vital Force to flow from the ends of the fingers into the affected part. In some cases, the best results may be obtained in this manner.

A variation of Digital Presentation may be effected by what is known as Rotary Presentation, which consists in holding the hands as above stated, for a moment or two, and then beginning a rotary movement of the hand (at the distance of six inches) from left to right, in the same direction as the hands of a watch. This is quite stimulating.

Another variation is what is known as Perforating, which is accomplished by giving the fingers a "twisting" movement, just as if they were boring holes in the body of the patient (at the distance of six inches). This movement is very stimulating, and stirs into activity parts that are sluggish or congested. It is apt to produce a feeling of warmth in the part treated.

We wish to call attention to the fact that these Presentation treatments, the different forms vary in force. For instance Palmar Presentation is the mildest form. Then comes Digital Presentation, which is considerably stronger. Then comes Rotary Presentation, which manifests a considerably higher degree of energy. Then comes Perforation, which is the strongest of all.

Very good results may be obtained in certain cases, by what is known as the Application, the Hands, which consists in merely placing the hands (the palms of the hands, of course), directly upon the flesh over the affected part, and holding them there for several moments. Them removing them, rub the palms briskly together and replace them on the part. Repeat this number of times, and marked results will be apparent. This is a favorite treatment for headaches, and in fact, may be used in the treatment of almost any form of trouble, changing the position of the hands in order to suit the emergencies of the case. In cases of neuralgia etc., this form of treatment is found valuable relieving the pain. Stroking is a form of treatment that is very beneficial in directing the circulation, and equalizing it when there appears to be a tendency toward imperfect circulation, etc. It has a sedative, soothing effect, and is a very good method to use in winding up, or terminating a treatment.

Stroking should be applied by bringing the tips of the fingers in a very light contact with the body of the patient, over the affected parts or over the entire body. It should always be performed in a downward, or outward direction, and never in an upward or inward direction. It should be performed in one direction only, and not to-and-from. The tips of the fingers are to be moved gently over the body, with a very light contact, not even the weight of the hand being allowed to bear upon the patient. "Lightness, gentleness, and airiness," are the words best describing the movement. A little practice will give the student the right movement.

If you desire to stroke the entire body of the patient, it is well to divide the process into two distinct treatments, *viz.*, (1) from the head down to the waist, and (2) from the waist down to the feet. In giving the general stroking treatment to the whole body, it is well to devote considerable attention to the chest, and abdominal region, in order that the organs be stimulated, and their "magnetism" equalized.

It is well, also, to remember that the old and tried principle of "Rubbing," is but another mode of communicating Vital Force, or Prana. This form of treatment is as old as the human race, and has been practiced in all times, and by all peoples. Alpini reports, in his work entitled, "De Medicinse Egyptiorum," that the Egyptian priests were adepts at certain mystical and medical rubbings, which form the treatment that was used by them in curing chronic diseases. Hippocrates held rubbings in high favor, and evidently employed them very frequently. He has written as follows: "A doctor ought to know many things; he should not be unacquainted with the benefits to be derived from rubbing. With its application quite contrary effects may be produced; it loosens stiff joints, and gives tone and strength to those which are relaxed." Celsus, nearly two thousand years ago, was a vigorous advocate of this method of treatment, and in his books he devotes much space to this form of

Vital treatment, and incidentally proves that it was known and practiced long before his time.

In ancient Rome, rubbing was a favorite form of treatment, and was employed regularly by the wealthy, in order to keep in good condition, a practice that is followed by many wealthy people of our own times, under the name of "massage," etc. Alexander of Tralles, a Greek physician of the sixth century, was an initiate in the "mystic rubbings," and incorporated it in his practice. He claimed that it helped to throw off morbid matter, and calmed the nervous system, and facilitated perspiration. He also held that it tended to calm convulsions, and was efficacious in a number of complaints. He wrote much on the subject, and agreed with Hippocrates that these "secret rubbings" should be imparted only to "sacred persons," and not allowed to become the property of the profane. Peter Borel, the physician to Louis XIII, of France, reports that one Degoust, a clerk of the court at Nismes, healed multitudes of people, by rubbing their limbs.

And in our own time, Massage is a deservedly popular form of treatment, and the new school of "Osteopathy" is growing in favor. In both these forms of practice, outside of any particular virtue due to the particular merits claimed by the respective practitioners, there is a great benefit derived by the transmitting of Vital Force from healer to patient, whether the practitioner admits this to be the case or not.

In Rubbing for the purpose of stimulating the parts by Vital Force, the healer should be gentle in his movements, force not being desirable or necessary, as the effect is gained by the passing of Vitality to the parts, not by the mere manipulation.

In applying this form of treatment, the palm of the hand, and the lower part of the fingers, should be used. The tips of the fingers, and the end of the thumb should be turned back. Healers having a fleshy lower part of the thumb, may use its palmar surface effectively in this treatment. The movements should be made downward. Some practitioners use a slightly different movement from that above indicated, inasmuch as they make a peculiar pressure with the flat ends of the fingers, following after the pressure of the palm of the hand. Students may follow either plan, as may seem preferable to them. Some healers claim to get the best results from this employment of the finger ends, while others carefully avoid the use of same. In each case it has been noticed, that the particular form of treatment is used because the healer feels that the Vital Force is best conveyed by his particular form of treatment. It seems to be a matter of "feeling" on the part of the healer, and this peculiar "feeling" is a safe rule to follow, and it manifests itself to all persons after they begin to give treatments.

Another form of treatment, known as Rotary Motion has been found to be very efficacious, by a number of healers. It consists in a circular rubbing movement of the hand and fingers (as above described), over the affected parts. The movements should always be made in the direction of the movement of the hands of a watch, and never in a reverse direction. This movement produces activity of the cells, and is useful in cases of sluggish functioning, etc.

Another form of treatment is known as kneading, and is found valuable in cases of stiffened muscles, rheumatism, etc., in which the trouble is local and not organic. Kneading is accomplished by grasping the muscles or tissues, and "working" them against the adjacent surfaces. It is composed of three different forms, *vie.*, Surface Kneading, Palmar Kneading, and Digital Kneading.

Surface Kneading is practically a "pinching" movement and consists in grasping the skin firmly between the thumb and forefinger, and then lifting it up a little, and then releasing it and letting it fly back to its normal condition. The two hands are used, alternately, the one picking up the skin as the other drops it, the surface being gone over in a systematic manner. This is quite a stimulating treatment, and is very beneficial in cases of poor circulation, etc. Palmar Kneading is performed with the whole hand. The healer grasps the flesh, or muscle, with the palm of his hand, with fingers close together, and the, thumb out. Do not use the thumb, but grasp the flesh between the palm of the hand, and the fingers, the lower part of the palm, called the "heel" of the hand, and the fleshy part of the thumb being used in the movement. Hold the flesh firmly, and do not allow it to slip. Knead deeply, so as to reach well into the muscles and flesh. The muscle or flesh should be thoroughly "worked," and yet not sufficiently to produce soreness. Do not use too much force, but be gentle and yet firm. Use the hands alternately. There are a number of variations of this movement, which will "come" to the healer as he practices. He will feel that his, hands are "alive," and he will feel instinctively the best way to impart that life.

Digital Kneading is performed by grasping the flesh between the finger and thumb and gently "rubbing" it against the other flesh, or bone. In cases where stimulation is thought advisable, one may give forms of Percussion treatment, of which several are here mentioned. In giving this treatment, the wrist should be kept flexible, and "loose," a stiff wrist being guarded against. The percussion should be elastic and springy, avoiding all roughness or bruising.

The first method of administering Percussion may be called the "pounding movement," which consists in striking the body with the inside flat surface of the half-closed fist, the heel of the hand and the closed ends of the fingers coming in contact with the flesh.

The second method of administering Percussion may be called the "slapping movement," which consists of a chopping movement of the hand, which is held open with the fingers held together, the blow being made with the little finger side of the hand the hand being likened to a butcher's cleaver employed in chopping. The fingers are held loosely together, coming together in a vibratory movement when the blow strikes.

The third method may be called the slapping method," in which the hand applies a "slapping" or "spanking" blow, the fingers being held rigid.

The fourth method may be called the "clapping method," in which the hand is held in a hollow shape, so as to give forth a hollow sound the position being similar to that employed by some people in a theatre when they wish to make a loud hollow sound with their hands, in applauding. A little practice will perfect one in this movement.

The fifth method, may be called the "tapping method," and consists in holding the tips of the fingers of each hand together, and then tapping the body, using the hands alternately.

A favorite method of administering Pranic or Vital Force treatments is what is known as the "Vibrational Treatment," and consists of a series of vibrating movements of the healer's hand. The fingers are usually employed in giving this treatment. The fingers are placed firmly over the part to be treated, and then a fine trembling or vibrating movement is communicated to the hand by the muscles of the arm.

The movement is acquired by practice, and is somewhat difficult at first. It is a most powerful form of treatment, and the patient feels it like a current of electricity. You must not press on the body with your wrist, and no more than the weight of the hand should be felt by the patient. When the Vibrational Treatment is properly applied, the vibrations should permeate the region treated, so that if the other hand be placed under the body, the vibrations should be perceptible. Some teachers have instructed their pupils in this form of treatment, by placing a glass of water on a table, and instructing the student to make the Vibrational movements on the table. When the proper motion is acquired the water will merely quiver in the centre, and not move from side to side. We urge the student to give the necessary time and attention to Vibrational Treatment, as when once acquired it will be found wonderfully efficacious.

The Breath Treatment has been used by many healers with wonderful effect. This form of treatment, also, has been known from prehistoric times. Arnobe informs us that the Egyptians used this method in the treatment of disease with great success, and some claimed that it was superior to stroking, or laying on of the hands. Mercklin, in his Tractatus Medicophyeis, tells of a case in which a young child, apparently lifeless, was restored to life and strength, by the breath of an old woman. Borel (who lived about 1650 A. D.) tells of a sect in one part of India who cured sickness by this method, and there are in India today certain priests who breathe on the sick, and seem to impart new life and vigor to them. Borel tells of another case in which a servant brought to life the apparently dead body of his master by breathing upon him, and adds, quaintly: "'Is it astonishing that the breath of man should produce such results, when we read that God breathed into the body of Adam to give him life? It is a fraction of this divine breath which even today can bring back health to the sick." In Spain there are persons called insalmadores, who heal by the saliva and by the breath.

There are two general methods employed by healers in Breath Treatment. The first is generally known as "Hot Insufflation," which consists in placing over the affected part a clean towel or napkin, and then pressing half-opened mouth close up to the body, so that the breath cannot escape. Then breath slowly but firmly, as if you were causing the breath to penetrate the body. The towel will become very warm, and the patient will plainly feel the heat. Another form of giving this treatment is to hold the lips at a distance of nearly an inch from the body, and to breathe on it just as one does in winter to warm his hands. The second plan consists in puckering up the lips, and blowing the breath from a distance of a foot or more, just as if you were trying to blow out a candle. This has a calming effect, and may even produce drowsiness. It is also useful in clearing a congested head, caused by overstudy, etc.

Treatment by the Eye, is also much in favor by some healers, who use it in the following manner. They allow their gaze to "sweep" over the persons or the affected part, and literally bathe the patient in their "rays."

Vital Force is oftentimes imparted by means of intermediate objects, such as handkerchiefs, etc., which have been "magnetized" or "treated" just as if the person themselves were being treated. To "treat" or "magnetize" an object, such as a handkerchief, etc., the healer must make the passes over it, until he "feels" that it is surcharged, then he may discontinue his efforts. The object when worn by the patient, seems to radiate its magnetism gradually until after several days it seems to be exhausted. Some magnetize the object by holding it between their hands for a time.

In giving the several treatments, it is well to always conclude by giving the Stroking Treatment, described above. This leaves the patient soothed and calmed down, and quieted. Never fail to "quiet down" the patient after a treatment. These things will soon come "intuitively" to the healer, and after all there is a something that cannot be taught except by one's own experience. And no two healers follow just the same methods. Do not be afraid to follow your intuitive sense in this direction.

CHAPTER VIII

PRANIC BREATHING

Pranic Breathing plays a very important part in Pranic Healing. It is the means or method whereby the supply of Prana , is increased, and whereby it may be distributed to the affected parts.

Pranic breathing is based on the unceasing vibration which is always in evidence throughout all nature. Everything is in constant vibration. There is no rest in the Universe. From planet to atom, everything is in motion and vibration. If even a tiny atom would cease to vibrate the balance of Nature would be disturbed. In and through incessant vibration the work of the Universe is performed. Force or Energy is constantly playing on Matter, producing the phenomena of life.

The atoms of the human body are in a state of constant vibration. Vibration and motion is everywhere in evidence in the human economy. The cells of the body are constantly to be destroyed, replaced, and changed. Change, change everywhere and always.

Rhythm pervades the universe. Everything from the greatest sun to the tiniest atom is in vibration, and has its own particular rate of vibration. The circling of the planets around the sun; the rise and fall of the sea ; the breathing of the heart ; the ebb and flow of the tide ; all follow rhythmic laws. All growth and change is in evidence of this law.

Our bodies are subject to this law, as well as are all other forms of matter. And on an understanding of this law of rhythm the Yogi theory of Breath, and Pranic Healing largely depends. By falling in with the rhythm of the atoms of which the body is composed, the Yogi manages to absorb a great amount of Prana, which he disposes of to bring about the results desired by him.

The body which you occupy is like a small inlet running in to the land from the sea. Although apparently subject only to its own laws, it is really subject to the ebb and flow of the tides of the ocean. The great sea of life is swelling and receding, rising and falling, and we are responding to its vibrations and rhythm. In a normal condition we receive the vibration and rhythm of the great ocean of life, and respond to it, but at times the month of the inlet seems choked np with debris, and we fail to receive the impulse from Mother Ocean, and in harmony manifests within us.

You have heard how a note on a violin, if sounded repeatedly and in rhythm, will start into motion vibrations which will in time destroy a bridge. The same result is true when a regiment of soldiers crosses a bridge, the order being always given to "break step" on such an occasion, lest the vibration bring down both bridge and regiment. These manifestations of the effect of rhythmic motion will give you an idea of the effect on the body of rhythmic breathing. The whole system catches the vibration and becomes in harmony with the will, which causes the rhythmic motion of the lungs, and while in such complete harmony will respond readily to orders from the will. With the body thus attuned, the Yogi finds no difficulty in increasing the circulation in any part of the body by an order from the will, and in the same way he can direct an increased current of nerve force to any part or organ, strengthening and stimulating it.

In the same way the Yogi by rhythmic breathing "catches the swing, " as it were, and is able to absorb and control a greatly increased amount of Prana, which is then at the disposal of his will. He can and does use it as a vehicle for sending forth Prana to others. Rhythmic breathing will increase the value of mental healing, magnetic healing, etc., several hundred per cent.

In rhythmic breathing the main thing to be acquired is the mental idea or rhythm. To those who know anything of music, the idea of measured counting is familiar. To others, the rhythmic step of the soldier; "Left right; left, right; left, right ; one, two, three, four; one, two, three, four," will convey the idea.

The Yogi bases his rhythmic time on a unit corresponding with the beat of his heart. The heart beat varies in different persons, but the heart beat unit of each person is the proper rhythmic standard for that particular individual is his rhythmic breathing. Ascertain your normal heart beat by placing your fingers over your pulse, and then count: "1, 2, 3, 4, 5, 6 ; 1, 2, 3, 4, 5, 6," etc., until the rhythm becomes firmly fixed in your mind. A little practice will fix the rhythm, so that you will be able to easily reproduce it. The beginner usually inhales in about six pulse units, but he will be able to greatly increase this by practice.

The Yogi rule for rhythmic breathing is that the units of inhalation and exhalation should be the same, while the units for retention and between breaths should be one-half the number of those of inhalation and exhalation.

The following exercises in Rhythmic Breathing should be thoroughly mastered, as it forms the basis of numerous other exercises, to which reference will be made later.

RHYTHMIC BREATHING

(1) Sit or stand, in an easy posture, being sure to hold the chest, neck and head as nearly in a straight line as possible, with shoulders slightly thrown back and hands resting easily on the lap. In this position the weight of the body is largely supported by the ribs and the position may be easily maintained. The Yogi has found that one cannot get the best effect of rhythmic breathing with the chest drawn in and the abdomen protruding.

(2) Inhale slowly a deep breath, counting six pulse units.

(3) Retain, counting three pulse units.

(4) Exhale slowly through the nostrils, counting six pulse units.

(5) Count three pulse beats between breaths.

(6) Repeat a number of times, but avoid fatiguing yourself at the start.

(7) When you are ready to close the exercise, practice the cleansing breath, which will rest you and cleanse the lungs.

After a little practice you will be able to increase the duration of the inhalations and exhalations, until about fifteen pulse units are consumed. In this increase, remember that the units for retention and between breaths is one half the units for inhalation and exhalation.

Do not overdo yourself in your effort to increase the duration of the breath, but pay as much attention as possible to acquiring the "rhythm," as that is more important than the length of the breath. Practice and try until you get the measured "swing" of the movement, and until you can almost "feel" the rhythm of the vibratory motion throughout your whole body. It will require a little practice and perseverance, but your pleasure at your improvement will make the task an easy one. The Yogis are most patient and persevering men, and their great attainments are due largely to the possession of these qualities.

The following will give you a general idea of the use of the breath in Pranic Healing :

GENERAL DIRECTIONS

The main principle to remember is that by rhythmic breathing and controlled thought you are enabled to absorb a considerable amount of Prana, and are also able to pass it into the body of another person, stimulating weakened parts and organs and imparting health and driving out diseased conditions. You must first learn to form such a clear mental image of the desired condition that you will be able to actually feel the influx of Prana, and the force running down your arms and out of your finger tips into the body of the patient. Breathe rhythmically a few times until the rhythm is fairly established, then place your hands on the affected part of the body of the patient, letting them rest lightly over the part. Then breathe rhythmically, holding the mental image that you are fairly "pumping" Prana into the diseased organ or part, stimulating it, and driving out the diseased conditions, just as one may pump clear water into a pail of dirty water, and thus drive out the latter in time. This plan is very effective if the mental image of the "pumping operation" is clearly held, the inhalation representing the lifting of the pump-handle, and the exhalation the actual pumping. In this way the patient is filled full of Prana and the diseased condition is driven out. Every once in a while raise the hands and snap the fingers as if you were throwing off the diseased condition. It is well to do this occasionally and also to wash the hands after treatment, as otherwise you may take on a trace of the diseased condition of the patient. During the treatment let the Prana pour into the patient in one continuous stream, allowing yourself to be merely the pumping machinery connecting the patient with the universal supply of Prana, and allowing it to flow freely through you. You need not work the hands vigorously, but simply enough that the Prana freely reaches the affected parts. The rhythmic breathing must be practiced frequently during the treatment, so as to keep the rhythm normal and to afford the Prana a free passage. It is better to place, the hands on the bare skin, but where this is not advisable or possible place them over the clothing. Vary above method occasionally during the treatment by stroking the body gently and softly with the finger tips, the fingers being kept slightly separated. This is very soothing to the patient, In cases of long standing you may find it helpful to give the mental command in words, such as "get out, get out," or "be strong, be strong, " as the case may be, the words helping you to exercise the will more forcibly and to the point. Vary these instructions to suit the needs of the case, and use your own judgment and inventive faculty. We have given you the general principles and you can apply them in hundreds of different ways. The above apparently simple instruction, if carefully studied, and applied, will enable one to accomplish all that the leading "magnetic healers " are able to, although their "systems" are more or less cumbersome and complicated. They are using Prana ignorantly and calling it "magnetism." If they would combine rhythmic breathing with their "magnetic" treatment they would double their efficiency.

CHAPTER IX

AUTO-PRANIC TREATMENTS

It is well to begin treatments by preparing the hands, as follows :

PREPARING THE HANDS

Rub the hands together briskly for a few minutes, and then swing them to-and-fro a little while, until they have that indefinable feeling of "aliveness" and being full of Energy. Clenching the hands together, and then opening them rapidly repeating several times will stimulate them wonderfully. Try it now, and see how the force seems to go to them. Some practitioners of Pranic Healing devote much of the time to what is known as the General Treatment, while others give the General Treatment only occasionally, and devote more time to the special treatments of the affected parts. But, at any rate, there is nothing better than a General Treatment given frequently, for it equalizes the circulation of the entire body, stimulates every muscle and nerve, and part, and causes the whole body to function with renewed energy and life, and aids materially in reestablishing normal conditions and functioning.

GENERAL TREATMENT

Place the patient on his face, placing a pillow under his breast so that his chin may rest easily upon it, letting him place his arms in a comfortable position, hanging by the sides preferably. Then place your first and second finger on each side of his spinal column, or "back-bone," so that the spine rests between the two fingers. Then bring the fingers down along the spine, slowly and firmly. If you find any tender joints you will know that some of the nerves emerging from the spinal column are congested, and that some organ or part is suffering by reason thereof. If you notice a point much colder or warmer than the neighboring points you will know that there is some muscular contraction in the spinal region, which is affecting the circulation of the nerve centers, thereby causing pain and abnormal action in some part of the body reached by the nerve. Remember these points so that you may treat them specially by careful manipulation and stimulating vibration. Then turn the patient over on his back and pass the hands over the entire body, in turn, noting all contraction, tender spots, swellings, etc.

Begin the actual general treatment by giving him a thorough spinal treatment as follows: Manipulate gently and carefully the entire length of the spinal column or back-bone, beginning at the neck, and working downward gradually, paying particular attention to the tender spots, or the points evidencing cold or heat, as before stated. First, work down one side of the spine, and then the other, manipulating carefully at each point. Then give him a vibration treatment along the spine, finishing with a gentle stroking, which will be found very soothing.

Then give him a Neck Treatment, as follows: Begin by a thorough kneading of the muscles of the back part of the neck, and a gentle manipulation of the throat. This treatment tends to render free and equal the circulation to and from the brain.

Then manipulate the shoulders and arms, in succession, finishing by stroking the arm from the shoulder down to the finger-tips.

Then manipulate the chest and back, and sides, in succession, finishing always with a Stroking. Apply Vibrations whenever the same seems advisable and comfortable to the patient. Apply percussion to the solid parts of the body when you deem it advisable.

Then give the legs the same treatment that you have given the arms, finishing always with Stroking.

Then give the special regions—that is, the regions affected by pain, and disease, the various treatments that seem advisable, following the instructions given in the preceding chapter. A good plan is to place the right hand over the pit of the stomach, or solar plexus, and the left hand under the middle of the back, and allow the current of Prana or Vital Force to flow through the body for a few minutes. In giving treatments in cases where pain is felt by the patient, heat your hands by briskly rubbing them together until they are well heated, and then place the right hand on the seat of the pain, and the left hand on the opposite side of the body or part, and mentally Will that the current shall drive out the pain. Always conclude the special or General Treatment with Stroking, which leaves the patient soothed and equalizes the circulation. You will be surprised at the wonderful effect of the Stroking.

In the manipulation during the General Treatment, pause occasionally and allow the hands to rest on the body, the right hand on the front of the body and the left hand on the back. This allows the current to flow freely through, reaching the parts.

CONSTIPATION

This trouble is treated by General Treatment, and special manipulations over the region of the Liver, and Abdomen. Vibration over the Liver and Bowels is also very efficacious in this case. Do not neglect the form of treatment whereby the current is passed through the parts, as stated above. Finish by Stroking. Be sure and advise the patient to drink more water, as Constipation is often caused by lack of sufficient fluids. Read the chapter on that subject in "Hatha Yoga."

DYSPEPSIA

This trouble is treated by General Treatment coupled with special treatments similar to that given in the case of Constipation, paying particular attention to the passing of the current through the digestive organs.

DIARRHEA

This trouble may be relieved, and sometimes almost instantaneously cured by Pranic Treatment. In treating for this trouble be very gentle and avoid manipulations, confining the movements to Stroking, passing the current through the parts, etc., coupled with the following *Special Treatment for Diarrhea*: This Special Treatment consists in an equalizing of the nerve force in what is known as the Splanchnic Nerve, which seems to have the faculty of occasionally "running-away" like a frightened horse. This Special Treatment brings a pressure to bear on this nerve, and seems to be brought to its senses, especially if the Mind of the healer is directed to the spot, with a firm command, "Slow, Down." The following is the best way to apply this treatment: Let the patient lie down on his back. Then place one hand under each side, placing your fingers on each side of his spine just below his last ribs. Then lift him up several inches, allowing his weight to rest on your fingers, his shoulders and "seat" resting on the bed, his back thus forming an arch. Do not be in a hurry, and move slowly. Let him relax all his muscles during the treatment. Let him rest for, say fifteen minutes, and then if the trouble has not disappeared give him another treatment. Finish the treatment with Stroking. You will be surprised at the quickness with which the trouble often disappears during this treatment. You must keep your mind on the subject during the treatment, sending out strong thoughts of "Slow Down."

LIVER TROUBLES are treated by General Treatments, accompanied with Special Treatments in the shape of manipulation of the region of the liver, accompanied with vibrations over the seat of the trouble. Do not forget to finish the treatment with Stroking.

KIDNEY TROUBLES are treated similar to Liver Troubles, except that the Special Treatments are given over the region of the Kidneys.

RHEUMATISM is treated by General Treatments accompanied by Special Kneading and manipulation of the affected part.

NEURALGIA is treated by General Treatment, accompanied by Special Kneading and manipulation of the affected part.

IMPOTENCY, on Sexual weakness, is treated by General Treatment and Special manipulation and vitalizing of the region of the lower part of the back-bone or spine and the upper part of the "seat".

FEMALE TROUBLES may be greatly benefitted by General Treatment, and a gentle Special treatment of the parts around the seat of the trouble, special attention being given to Vibration over the parts.

GENERAL REMARKS ON TREATMENTS

The above forms of treatments are given merely as a general guide. The healer must be governed by that sense of "Intuition" that comes to all healers who are interested in their work, and seems to be a special sense which Nature has bestowed upon those having an earnest desire to "heal". This will come to you, and you will then understand it much better than we could tell you. The first thing to do is to THOROUGHLY acquaint yourself with each and every one of the forms of treatment described in the last chapter, so that you can make each movement naturally and easily, just as you use your hands in carrying your food to your mouth; in dressing yourself, etc., etc. Then when you have acquired the movements in this way when they have become second- nature, as it were then you will find yourself feeling impelled to use certain motions and movements, in preference to others, in each case, and you will find that the requirements of each case are met much better in this way than by the following of any set rules or directions in any book, or from any teacher. There is a "Healing Sense" that is just as real as any other of the senses, as you will discover if you get into this work. But remember this, acquaint yourself thoroughly with the details of each and every particular movement and form of treatment. Practice on some friend or relative, who is willing to help you. A few minutes actual practice in this way, is worth pages of directions. Have confidence in yourself, and the Power that flows through you, and you will be successful.

DISTANT HEALING

Prana colored by the thought of the sender may be projected to persons at a distance, who are willing to receive it, and the healing work done in this way. This is the secret of the "absent healing" of which the Western world has heard so much of late years. The thought of the healer sends forth and colors the Prana of the sender, and it flashes across space and finds lodgment in the psychic mechanism of the patient. It is unseen, and like the Marconi waves, it passes through intervening obstacles and seeks the person attuned to receive it. In order to treat persons, at a distance, you must form a mental image of them until you can feel yourself to be en rapport with them. This is a psychic process dependent upon the mental imagery of the healer. You can feel the sense of rapport when it is established, it manifesting in a sense of nearness. That is about as plain as we can describe it. It may be acquired by a little practice, and some will get it at the first trial.

When rapport is established, say mentally to the distant patient, "I am sending you a supply of Vital Force or power, which will invigorate you and heal you. Then picture the Prana as leaving your mind with each exhalation of rhythmic breath, and traveling across space instantaneously and reaching the patient and healing him. It is not necessary to fix certain hours for treatment, although you may do so if you wish. The receptive condition of the patient, as he is expecting and opening himself up to your psychic force, attunes him to receive your vibrations whenever you may send them. If you agree upon hours, let him place himself in a relaxed attitude and receptive condition. The above is the great underlying principle of he "absent treatment" of the Western world. You may do these things as well as the noted healers, with a little practice.

CHAPTER X

AUTO-PRANIC TREATMENTS

Not only is it possible for one person to treat another by Pranic Force, but one may also treat himself or herself with considerable effect, in the same way. This may seem strange at first thought, for the underlying principle of Pranic Healing seems to be that the healer sends a supply of Pranic Force to the affected parts, supplying the deficiency of Prana in those parts. This is true, but when it is remembered that one may draw Prana from the Universal Supply, and then distribute the same to the parts, it will be seen that one may treat himself by this method. In fact, it is claimed by some that the deficiency of Prana lies in the fact that it is not equally distributed, from some state of contraction or congestion, and that the real process of Pranic Healing consists in an equalization, or distribution of the Prana throughout the system. At any rate everyone may benefit himself or herself by giving auto or self -Pranic treatments.

In order to give these treatments correctly, one should acquaint himself with the movements or forms of treatment mentioned in our previous chapters, relating to the treatment of others by the Pranic method, and should then endeavor to reproduce these movements on themselves. Beginning, with the Pranic Breathing, the person should fill his nerve centers full of fresh Prana, and then to proceed to redistribute it throughout his system in the way of a General Treatment, following up the same by a special treatment of the affected parts. It is wonderful how much good one may do himself in this way, and how invigorated and strong he will feel after such a treatment.

Of course, one cannot treat himself as "handily" as he could treat another, for the reason that he cannot "handle" himself as well, but a little practice, and the exercise of a little ingenuity in the application of the treatments, will do wonders.

The manipulations, kneading, stroking, vibration treatment, and many of the other forms and degrees of treatment, may be successfully administered by one's self. We do not think it necessary to go into details of this treatment here, for this would be but a repetition of the forms of treatment given in the previous chapters. All that we can say is that If you will acquaint yourself thoroughly with the directions given in the said chapters, you will have at your command a mighty source of relief and cure, that you may be in danger of overlooking simply because of its "simplicity" and "plainness". We have known of many persons who have treated themselves successfully in this way, and we see no reason why anyone cannot do likewise. The best instruction that we can give you is to START IN AND DO IT, according to the directions already given. Do not neglect the breathing exercises, as that lies at the basis of the entire treatment.

Now, this chapter is short, and many of you may not attach to it the importance that you would grant it if it were "padded out." But we assure you that if you read it carefully you will find that it contains a hint of a very valuable and important truth, which hint, if taken, may lead to wonderful results. The plainest things are often the most valuable, but, alas! we neglect them because they are so plain and simple, and run after some other things, not half so good, simply because they seem more complex and wonderful. Do not make this mistake, friends.

The following exercises will be found most useful in Auto-Pranic Healing:

PRANA DISTRIBUTING

Lying flat on the floor or bed, completely relaxed, with hands resting lightly over the Solar Plexus (over the pit of the stomach, where the ribs begin to separate), breathe rhythmically. After the rhythm is fully established will that each inhalation will draw in an increased supply of Prana or vital energy from the Universal supply, which will be taken up by the nervous system and stored in the Solar Plexus. At each exhalation will that the Prana or vital energy is being distributed all over the body, to every organ and part; to every muscle, cell and atom; to nerve, artery and vein; from the top of your head to the soles of your feet; invigorating, strengthening and stimulating every nerve; recharging every nerve center; sending energy, force and strength all over the system. While exercising the will, try to form a mental picture of the inrushing Prana, coming in through the lungs and being taken up at once by the Solar Plexus, then with the exhaling effort, being sent to all parts of the system, down to the finger tips and down to the toes. It is not necessary to use the Will with an effort. Simply commanding that which you wish to produce and then making the mental picture of it is all that is necessary. Calm command with the mental picture is far better than forcible willing, which only dissipates force needlessly. The above exercise is most helpful and greatly refreshes and strengthens the nervous system and produces a restful feeling all over the body. It is especially beneficial in cases where one is tired or feels a lack of energy.

INHIBITING PAIN

Lying down or sitting erect, breathe rhythmically, holding the thought that you are inhaling Prana. Then when you exhale, send the Prana to the painful part to re-establish the circulation and nerve current. Then inhale more Prana for the purpose of driving out the painful condition; then exhale, holding the thought that you are driving out the pain. Alternate the two above mental commands, and with one exhalation stimulate the part and with the next drive out the pain. Keep this up for seven breaths, then rest a while. Then try it again until relief comes, which will be before long. Many pains will be found to be relieved before the seven breaths are finished. If the hand is placed over the painful part, you may get quicker results. Send the current of Prana down the arm and into the painful part.

DIRECTING THE CIRCULATION

Lying down or sitting erect, breathe rhythmically, and with the exhalations direct the circulation to any part you wish, which may be suffering from imperfect circulation. This is effective in cases of cold feet or in cases of headache, the blood being sent downward in both cases, in the first case warming the feet, and in the latter, relieving the brain from too great pressure. In the case of headache, try the Pain Inhibiting first, then follow with sending the blood downward. You will often feel a warm feeling in the legs as the circulation moves downward. The circulation is largely under the control of the will and rhythmic breathing renders the task easier.

PSYCHIC HEALING

GENERAL SELF-HEALING

Lying in a relaxed condition, breathe rhythmically, and command that a good supply of Prana be inhaled. With the exhalation, send the Prana to the affected part for the purpose of stimulating it. Vary this occasionally by exhaling, with the mental command that the diseased condition be forced out and disappear. Use the hands in this exercise, passing them down the body from the head to the affected part. In using the hands in healing yourself or others always hold the mental image that the Prana is flowing down the arm and through the finger tips into the body, thus reaching the affected part and healing it. Of course we can give only

81

general directions in this book without taking up the several forms of disease in detail, but a little practice of the above exercise, varying it slightly to fit the conditions of the case, will produce wonderful results. Some Yogis follow the plan of placing both hands on the affected part, and then breathing rhythmically, holding the mental image that they are fairly pumping Prana into the diseased organ and part, stimulating it and driving out diseased conditions, as pumping into a pail of dirty water will drive out the latter and fill the bucket with, fresh, water. This last plan is very effective if the mental image of the pump is clearly held, the inhalation representing the lifting of the pump handle and the exhalation the actual pumping.

RECHARGING YOURSELF

If you feel that your vital energy is dwindling, and that you need to store up a new supply quickly, the best plan is to place the feet close together (side by side, of course) and to lock the fingers of both hands in any way that seems the most comfortable. This closes the circuit, as it were, and prevents any escape of Prana through the extremities. Then breathe rhythmically a few times, and you will feel the effect of the recharging.

BRAIN STIMULATING

The Yogis have found the following exercise most useful in stimulating the action of the brain for the purpose of producing clear thinking and reasoning. It has a wonderful effect in clearing the brain and nervous system, and those engaged in mental work will find it most useful to them, both in the direction of enabling them to do better work and also as a means of refreshing the mind and clearing it after arduous mental labor.

Sit in an erect posture, keeping the spinal column straight, and the eyes well to the front, letting the hands rest on the upper part of the legs. Breathe rhythmically, but instead of breathing through both nostrils as in the ordinary exercises, press the left nostril close with the thumb, and inhale through the right nostril. Then remove the thumb, and close the right nostril with the finger, and then exhale through the left nostril. Then, without changing the fingers, inhale through the left nostril, and changing fingers, exhale through the right. Then inhale through right and exhale through left, and so on, alternating nostrils as above mentioned, closing the unused nostril with the thumb or forefinger. This is one of the oldest forms of Yogi breathing, and is quite important and valuable, and is well worthy of acquirement.

THE GRAND YOGI PSYCHIC BREATH

The Yogis have a favorite form of psychic breathing which they practice occasionally, to which has been given a Sanskrit term of which the above is a general equivalent. We have given it last, as it requires practice on the part of the student in the line of rhythmic breathing and mental imagery, which he has now acquired by means of the preceding exercises. The general principles of the Grand Breath may be summed up in the old Hindu saying: "Blessed is the Yogi who can breathe through his bones." This exercise will fill the entire system with Prana, and the student will emerge from it with every bone, muscle, nerve, cell, tissue, organ and part energized and attuned by the Prana and the rhythm of the breath. It is a general housecleaning of the system, and he who practices it carefully will feel as if he had been given a new body, freshly created, from the crown of his head to the tips of his toes. We will let the exercise speak for itself.

(1) Lie in a relaxed position, at perfect ease.

(2) Breathe rhythmically until the rhythm is perfectly established.

(3) Then, inhaling and exhaling, form the mental image of the breath being drawn up through the bones of the legs, and then forced out through them;

then through the bones of the arms; then through the top of the skull; then through the stomach; then through the reproductive region; then as if it were traveling upward and downward along the spinal column; and then as if the breath were being inhaled and exhaled through every pore of the skin, the whole body being filled with Prana and life.

(4) Then (breathing rhythmically) send the current of Prana to the Seven Vital Centers, in turn, as follows, using the mental picture as in previous exercises:

(a) To the forehead

(b) To the back of the head

(c) To the base of the brain

(d) To the Solar Plexus

(e) To the Sacral Region (lower part of the spine)

(f) To the region of the navel

(g) To the reproductive region

Finish by sweeping the current of Prana, to and fro, from head to feet several times.

CHAPTER XI

THOUGHT-FORCE HEALING

Before passing on to the various forms of Mental Healing, proper, we must acquaint ourselves with a form of healing—and a very efficacious one too—that comes in between Pranic Healing and Mental Healing. This form of healing is known by a number of names, but we have thought it well to give it the name "Thought-force Healing", which describes it very well, for it is an application of Thought and Prana. In our "Fourteen Lessons" we have shown you how Thought could color the Prana, and go forth as an almost living Energy. This "Thought-force," as it is called, may be employed as a means of Healing, and in fact we have known of a number of very able practitioners who preferred it to any other form, because of its simplicity and power. It may be used either as a separate system, or else in connection with one or more of the other systems mentioned in this book. In fact, the better Psychic Healers use parts of all methods, adapting the same to meet the several requirements of their patients, giving preference to those forms which seemed "most natural" to the healer, and the patient.

Thought-force healing is based on the fact that the organs, parts, and even cells of the body have "mind" in them a fact known to all occultists, and which modern science fully recognizes. This "mind" in the cells, cell-groups, nerve centers, ganglia, etc., respond to a strong thought impression from outside, particularly when the thought is heavily charged with Prana. The parts are thus reached directly, rather than through the Instinctive mind, as is the case in Mental Healing, proper. When properly applied this form of Healing produces a wonderfully quick and direct effect, and therefore it is one of the simplest and best forms of general psychic treatment. The student is advised to acquaint himself thoroughly with it.

The central theory of Thought-force healing is that the disease is a mental trouble not a trouble in the central mind, but in the "mind" in the parts. The theory of the cure is that the Thought-force overcomes the rebellious "mind" in the cells and parts, and forces it to resume normal action.

In Thought-force healing, get all ideas of "matter" out of your mind. You are not using Mind against Matter, but Mind against Mind. The Will-Mind against the cell-mind. Do not forget this, for it underlies the whole system of treatment. The healer goes after the rebellious "mind" in the parts remember that. By producing, or rather re-establishing normal mental conditions in the parts, the diseased condition vanishes.

The Healer directs his Thought-force to the "mind" in the part, and addresses it positively, either by uttering the actual words or by speaking them mentally. He thinks, or speaks, some thing like this: "Now, MIND, you are behaving badly you are acting like a spoiled child you know better, and I expect you to do better. You must, and will do better, and act right. You must bring about normal and healthy conditions. You have charge of these organs, and I expect you to do the work that the Infinite Mind gave you to do properly. This and similar thoughts will give you the idea of the treatment. Point out to the "mind" of the part, just what you expect it to do. And you will be surprised (at first) at how readily the cell-mind obeys. The rebellious mind of the parts acts like a child who is "pouty," "cross," or "out-of-sorts." It must be coaxed, scolded, led, or loved into right action, as the case seems to require — the idea of Love, of course, being behind it all, just as in the case of the child. The cell-mind is essentially an undeveloped, child-like mind, and if you keep this idea in view, you will be able to apply the treatment to the best advantage. As you will see as we proceed, the hands are used in this form of treatment, but principally for the purpose of "attracting the attention" of the mind in the cells and parts, just as we attract the attention of a man by tapping him on the shoulder, etc. Awaken the "attention" of the cell-mind, and you will find that your orders are listened to carefully.

There is a great difference in the quality in the mind in the several organs, just as in the case of different children. For instance the heart is very intelligent, and responds readily to commands from the central mind. The liver, on the other hand, is a "stupid," dense, mental organism, and needs to be "driven" like a mule, instead of lead like a lamb. You have seen children just like this carry this idea in your mind. Now yon have had the theory let us go into the practice of Thought-force Healing.

PRACTICE

STOMACH TROUBLES

The majority of diseases really originate in the Stomach, and the other troubles are really but resultants of the main trouble which is in the Stomach. Consequently, it is well to always begin the treatment with a Stomach treatment. Indigestion and malnutrition are at the bottom of nine-tenths of the various diseases. Remove the cause and the symptoms disappear.

The method of treating the mind in the Stomach is as follows: Have the patient standing erect in front of you, or else lying down on his back. Then give him several quick (but gentle) taps or pats of the hand over the Stomach, saying "Mind, wake up!" Then hold the palm of the right hand over the Stomach, saying to the latter: "Now Stomach-mind, I want you to wake up, and attend to this organ properly. You have not been doing right. You have been neglecting your work. I want you to begin functioning properly, and making the organ strong, healthy, and active. I want it to do its work properly, and you must see that it does so. You must see that it digests the food properly, and nourishes the whole body. You must relieve the congestion and inactivity, and see that the whole organ acts with life and energy, and does its work well." You need not repeat these exact words, and you may add or vary the same. The main thing is to tell the Stomach-mind just what you expect it to do, and what you look to it to bring about. You will be surprised at the intelligence displayed by the mind addressed, and how quickly it begins to act upon your instructions.

Give stomach treatments daily. The treatment should last about five to ten minutes. It usually takes from one to four weeks to get final results in cases of

Dyspepsia, the difference depending upon the length of standing of the trouble, and the mental attitude of the patient, that is whether he works with you or against you.

LIVER TROUBLES

Treat the Liver in a similar manner to that given to the Stomach. The Liver, however, being a dull, stupid organ, must be spoken to sharply and positively—think of a stubborn donkey, and you have the idea. The liver cannot be coaxed it must be driven like a mule. "When we speak of the Liver, we mean the "Mind" of the Liver, of course. Give the Liver instructions to function properly; to secrete the proper amount of bile, and no more; to let the bile flow freely and perform its work, etc.

CONSTIPATION

Treat Constipation, by first treating the Liver, as above directed. Then pass the hand over the bowels, saying "Bowel-mind, wake up attend to your duties move naturally and easily, as you know you should do." Constipation is sometimes rendered stubborn by a tendency to contraction on the part of the anus (the posterior outer opening of the colon or large bowel, through which the excrement passes when one has "a movement", or "passage"). In such cases, place the hand over the part (outside of the clothing will answer) pressing the part a little to attract its attention, and saying to it "relax, relax you are causing trouble. Relax, and allow the movements to pass freely and naturally."

DIARRHEA

Diarrhea is treated similarly to Constipation, the same organs being treated, the directions being reversed, of course. The Bowel is told to "slow down", and the Liver is told to behave itself.

KIDNEYS

The Kidneys are treated in a similar manner to the Liver. Tap them smartly with the fingers, several times, and then tell them to do their work properly, and naturally. In cases where the patient urinates too freely, instruct the kidneys and bladder to "slow down", and endeavor to reduce the urination gradually. If the patient is in the habit of getting up three times during the night, bring him down to two times, then to one time, and then to no urination at all between bedtime and morning. Treat daily, from five to ten minutes. Continue treatments for a month in treatment for excessive urination, it is well to add upward passes along the region, holding the mental picture of pushing back the flow. These upward passes are also good to use in case of Diarrhea in addition to the regular treatment.

RHEUMATISM

Rheumatism is treated in two ways, combined. The first treatment is given to the Kidneys, the Kidney-mind being instructed to eliminate the impurities and uric acid, and discharge it from the system. The failure to do this is the main cause of Rheumatism, and it follows that a correction of the original trouble will bring about good results, and prevent a recurrence of the trouble. At the same time, the parts affected should be manipulated, and at the same time addressed and told to throw off and get rid of the uric acid, and to relax and allow contraction to be thrown off. Treat the stomach also, for much of the original trouble comes from malnutrition, and imperfect digestion.

HEART TROUBLES

The heart is the most intelligent of the organs that is it has a higher grade of "mind" in it, than any organ (the brain excepted, of course). This Heart-mind will respond readily to loving instructions, and is most gentle and kind. In case the heart is palpitating or beating irregularly, place the hand gently over the part, and say kindly, "Heart-mind, quiet down quiet, quiet, quiet, act regularly, and quietly steady, steady, steady," etc. You will find that the palpitation will gradually quiet down and the heart's action will become steady and regular.

THE NERVES

Nervous troubles may be treated in this way. Commence with treating the Stomach, and Liver, and getting them to function properly. Then treat the nerves along the spinal column, giving them the appropriate instructions, to suit the requirements of the case.

EQUALIZING THE CIRCULATION

This is accomplished by making long sweeping passes from the head to the feet (see Pranic Healing, for direction) at the same time saying to the "mind" of the arteries and veins "flow freely, and equally steadily and constantly flow, circulate, flow." It is well to give this treatment for Equalizing the Circulation, in nearly every form of treatment, since by doing so you will help to re-establish normal conditions, and promote the return of healthy action.

HEADACHES

Headaches are treated by first treating the Stomach, and then Equalizing the Circulation, and then giving local treatments to the Head, saying to the "mind" of the parts: " quiet down, now, easy, easy, easy, rest, rest, rest," etc.

FEMALE TROUBLES

These complaints are treated by first restoring proper conditions of the Stomach, so that the patient may be properly nourished, and may thus obtain energy and strength to send to the affected parts. This must not be overlooked. Local treatment is administered as in cases of Diarrhea, bring up the hands in front of the lower part of the abdomen, and giving the command to the "mind" Strength, right action, health, etc. In case of profuse flow, add the words: Slow down, cease flooding," etc. In the case of falling of the womb, etc., the command: "Firm, firm, now, firm," etc., will be found to have a wonderfully strengthening effect.

OTHEE COMPLAINTS

It is not necessary to run over the list of so called Diseases, which are after all nothing but different cases of imperfect "mind action." The treatment is similar in each case as you will have seen. Give the same general treatment, and then give your mental commands in words suited to the case. That is, tell the mind of the part what it must do. Talk to it just as you would to a child that was not doing what it should. Reason with it, and lead or drive it along, just as seems best. Use judgment and a little thought, and you will find that you will soon get the "knack" of giving just the right commands.

But, above everything else, remember that you are talking to the MIND of the part, not to dead matter. There is no dead matter about a live body — mind is in every part and cell. It is mind talking to mind, remember this, for therein lies the secret of this form of treatment.

Remember, also, that the majority of diseases arise from Stomach troubles and imperfect circulation. Restore the Stomach to normal action and the Circulation to equalize activity and functioning, and you have removed the cause of the trouble. Do not forget this for it is most important.

Talk to the mind as you would to a person, a child,

and say to it just what you think will best affect it. A little practice will render you very expert in this, and you will soon begin to feel quite well acquainted with the different forms of mind in the parts, and moreover they will soon begin to recognize that you know them, just as a horse recognizes men who are used to managing horses, although they may never have seen that particular man before. Dogs are the same way, as one will see if he will think a little bit. This form of treatment may be used on animals as well as on people, and we have heard of many remarkable cures in this way.

Now, remember, please, that the cell-mind, or part-mind does not understand the "words" you say — they have no such knowledge. But they *do* understand the thought that lies back of the words, and will respond thereto. The words only serve to help you to *form your thought dearly*. Words are but symbols of thoughts — there is one or more thoughts back of every word. Do yon see now? A German may give the treatment to an Englishman, who does not understand a single word used. But the cell-mind does understand the thought back of the word, no matter what language is spoken. Is not this wonderful? And yet, so simple, when the key is had. It is the thought, not the word. And, yet the spoken word helps the mind to form the thought. We think in words, remember. We even dream in words.

Now, do not let this simple form of treatment escape your attention. It is one of the best, for it combines the qualities of several others in it. It is so simple, and easily understood, and easily applied. Do not fail to try it.

AUTO-TREATMENT

This treatment may be administered to one's self, with the best possible effect. The Central Mind will give the command to the cell-mind or part-mind, just as in the case of treating another person. The methods used are practically the same as those above given. In fact, one may get a good idea of the treatments by " trying them on himself. "

It would be possible to write an entire book upon this subject of Auto-healing by Thought-force, but it would be merely a "padding out" of what has been given you in this chapter. Our idea, in this book, is to give you the best information in the shortest time, and smallest space. Each chapter gives you information that is worth many times the price of the book, and for which some who have acquired a knowledge of it are charging "tuition fees," ranging from hundreds of dollars upward. Many "courses" on the market contain no more information than is given in some of these chapters. "We say this not in a spirit of self-praise, but merely that you may understand that you are getting "the thing in a nutshell."

CHAPTER XII

SUGGESTIVE HEALING

Suggestive Healing is based on the effect of Mental Influence on the Instinctive Mind. It holds that just as the adverse suggestion of another, or of one's self, may produce abnormal conditions of the body, through the Instinctive Mind, so may the good suggestions of another, or one's self restore normal conditions.

The effect of the mental states on the body is well known to those who have examined into the matter, as well among physical scientists as among occultists. We cite or quote a few instances here, in order to call your attention to the facts underlying Suggestive Healing.

Prof. James, the eminent psychologist, has said: "The fact is that there is no sort of consciousness whatever, be it sensation, feeling or idea, which does

100

not directly and of itself tend to discharge into some motor effect. The motor effect need not always be an outer stroke of behavior. It may be only an alteration of the heartbeats or breathing, or a modification in the distribution of the blood, such as blushing or turning pale; or what not. But in any case, it is there in some shape when any consciousness is there; and a belief as fundamental as any in modern psychology, is the belief at last attained, that conscious processes of any sort, conscious processes merely as such, *must* pass over into motion open or concealed."

Bain says: "There have occurred many instances of death, or mental derangement, from a shock of grief, pain, or calamity; this is in accordance with the general law".

Darwin says: "In protracted grief the circulation becomes languid; the face pale; the muscles flaccid; the eyelids droop; the head hangs on the contracted chest; the lips, cheeks, and lower jaw all sink downward from their own weight. The whole expression of a man in good spirits is exactly opposite of the one suffering from sorrow. "

Olston says : "If the general law of the body be that of cheer, hope, joy, love, and desire for health and happiness give growth to tissue, strong and normal action to the organs of the body, and thereby health in general; while fear, melancholy, malice, hatred, dejection, loss of confidence and all other morbid states of mind tend to the lassitude of the functions and the depletion of the organs I feel that too much enthusiasm cannot be raised in the reader's mind upon these all important facts."

Flammarion says: "An idea, an impression, a mental commotion, while entirely internal, can produce in another direction physiological effects more or less intense, and is even capable of causing death. Examples are not wanting of persons dying suddenly in consequence of emotion. The power which imagination is capable of exercising over life has long been established. The experiment performed in the last century of a man condemned to death, who was made the subject of a study by medical men, is well known. The subject of the experiment was fastened securely to a table with strong straps, his eyes were bandaged, and he was then told that he was to be bled from the neck until every drop of his blood had been drained. After this an insignificant puncture was made in his "skin with the point of a needle, and a siphon arranged near his head in such a manner as to allow a stream of water to flow over his neck and fall with a slight sound to a basin placed on the floor. At the end of six minutes the condemned man, believing that he had lost at least seven or eight quarts of blood, died in terror."

Maudsley says: "Emotion may undoubtedly favor, hinder, or pervert nutrition, and increase, lessen, or alter a secretion; in doing which there is reason to think that it acts, not only by dilating or contracting the vessels through the vasomotor system, as we witness in the blush of shame and the pallor of fear, but also directly on the organic elements of the parts through the nerves, which, as the latest researches seem to show, end in them sometimes by continuity of substance. To me it seems not unreasonable to suppose that the mind may stamp its tone, if not its very features, on the individual elements of the body, inspiring them, with hope and energy, or inflicting them with despair and feebleness."

Darwin has told of the effect of grief on the physical functioning, particularly on the circulation. Homesickness is mentioned as apt to derange the proper functioning of the body. Good news will promote digestion; bad news will retard it. A disgusting sight will cause nausea.

Sir Samuel Baker says: "Any severe grief or anger is almost certain to be succeeded by fever in certain parts of Africa."

Sir B. W. Richardson says: "Diabetes from sudden mental shock is a true, pure type of a physical malady of mental origin."

Sir George Paget says: "In many cases I have seen reasons for believing that cancer has its origin in prolonged anxiety."

Murchison says: "I have been surprised how often patients with primary cancer of the liver have traced the cause of this illness to protracted grief or anxiety. The cases have been far too numerous to be accounted for as mere coincidences".

Numerous medical authorities report that cases of cancer especially of uterine cancer or cancer of the breast have their origin in mental anxiety. And other report cases of jaundice arising from the same cause. Other attribute anaemia to mental shock and worry.

Sir B. W. Richardson says: "Eruptions on the skin will follow excessive mental strain. In all of these and in cancer epilepsy and mania from mental causes there is a predisposition. It is remarkable how little the question of physical disease from mental influences has been studied. "

Prof. Elmer Gates says: "My experiments show that irascible malevolent and depressing emotions generate in the system injurious compounds some of which, are extremely poisonous; also that agreeable happy emotions generate chemical compounds of nutritious value, which stimulate the cells to manufacture energy."

Prof. Tuke, in his book, "The Influence of the Mind on the Body," cites numerous cases of disease caused by fear, worry or fright, the principal ones being as follows: insanity, idiocy, paralysis of various muscles and organs, profuse perspiration, cholerine, jaundice, turning the hair grey, baldness, decay of the teeth, nervous shock followed by fatal anaemia, uterine troubles, skin diseases, erysipelas, eczema, etc. The same authority remarks on the effect of fear in the spread of diseases, particularly contagious diseases. Cholera epidemics are believed to have been largely due to the fear of the people in former times.

Prof. Mosso claims that fear causes St. Vitus' dance, scurvy, epilepsy, etc.

Many writers have gone so far as to claim that Fear, in some form or degree was at the bottom of all physical complaints or diseases, directly or indirectly, and making allowance for over-claim, it looks as if there was much truth in the statement.

SUGGESTIVE HEALING

In view of the preceding, it would appear that any method of relieving or driving away Fear, would have a great effect in the curing of disease. And such is the case. Nearly all forms of Psychic Healing create a new mental atmosphere and condition in the patient. Fear is replaced by Confidence, Courage, Fearlessness, Hope, and the physical results follow. The axiom of Suggestive Therapeutics is "Thought takes form in Action "and "As a Man thinketh in his heart, so is he."

But not only may the entire system be benefited by general suggestion, but particular organs may be strengthened, and caused to again function properly, by well directed Suggestions. The Instinctive Mind takes up the suggestions passed on to it, and they "take form in action." The very cells of the body respond to Suggestion through the Instinctive Mind. And every part, organ, nerve, and cell may be strengthened and stimulated into proper action in this way.

The practice of Suggestive Therapeutics has proven quite popular among physicians of late years, and is destined under one form or another to rapidly increase in popular favor in the future. Many physicians give what are called "masked suggestions", by which is meant Suggestions given in connection with some material remedy, the patient being told positively that the drug or treatment will do "thus and so," and the suggestion being repeated in different forms, until the mind of the patient confidently expects the stated results, and the "Thought takes form in action." No matter how the Suggestion is given it is still Suggestion.

In the succeeding chapters we shall give special directions regarding this form of treatment, which will give one a better working knowledge than a book-full of mere general remarks. Study them carefully.

CHAPTER XIII

PRACTICE OF SUGGESTIVE HEALING

In our last chapter we showed how the Body might be affected by Mental States—how the Mind affected the physical being, through the medium of the Instinctive Mind. And, we have called your attention to the fact that just as the physical condition might be, adversely affected by mental conditions, so might it be favorably affected in the same way. Health is contagious as well as Disease, and "As a man thinketh in his heart, so is he," applies as well to Right-thinking as to Wrong-thinking. And upon this theory or fact, is based the practice of Suggestive Therapeutics.

The task before the practitioner of Suggestive Therapeutics is that of restoring normal mental conditions to those who have dropped into the habit of abnormal thinking about their bodies; and also to bring about normal conditions by means of the influence of the mind over the cells and parts composing the body. As we have stated, the principal difference between the practice of Mental Healing, and Suggestive Therapeutics consists in the manner of applying the treatment. In Mental Healing, there is little or no verbal suggestions, the healing work being done along the lines of Thought-transference or Telepathy. But in Suggestive Therapeutics, the treatment is given to the mind of the patient by means of verbal suggestions or words of the healer. Of course, even in Suggestive treatment the Thought of the healer operates directly on the mind of the patient, along the lines of Mental Healing, as well as by means of the verbal suggestion. The average Suggestionist will not admit this fact, but it is true nevertheless, and in fact it has very much to do with the cure. The verbal suggestion is often necessary in order to make the deep impression on the minds of some patients, but the healing mental force goes along with the suggestions, whether or not the healer is conscious of it. The fact that there is a great difference in the work of several suggestionists, in spite of the fact that they are all following the same method and even using the same words, will go toward proving this idea.

Now, right here at the beginning, in order that there may be no misunderstanding, let us say that

Suggestive Therapeutics, pure and simple, has no connection with Hypnotic Suggestion or Hypnotism. Of course, there are suggestionists who combine the two, but there is no use in it, and much to be urged against it. Hypnotism plays no real part in the practice of Suggestive Therapeutics. Hypnotists have found that when they obtained the hypnotic condition, they could suggest Health to their patients with effect, and they naturally supposed that hypnosis was a necessary precedent to the treatment and cure. But investigators have proven that the suggestions are just as effective when given to the patient when he is wide awake and conscious, and when there is no attempt to produce a condition of hypnosis. We urge our readers to divorce the idea of Hypnosis from that of Suggestive Therapeutics, in their minds. There is no real connection between them, and there are many, reasons why they should not be confounded with each other.

And, now that we have formed an idea of what Suggestive Therapeutics may do, and what it is, let us turn our attention to the methods of applying the treatment.

Receptivity of the Patient

The best results in giving Suggestive treatments are

obtained when the patient is induced to manifest a receptive attitude of condition of mind. Just as when one wishes to talk earnestly to another about some matter of importance, he seeks to have his hearer in a quiet, thoughtful mood, rather than in the midst of worries perplexities, business cares, etc., when his attention is diverted away from the subject under discussion just so should the healer endeavor to have his patient maintain a calm, relaxed, peaceful frame of mind during the treatment.

Attention

The patient should be induced to give the healer his entire attention, as the measure of the effect of the treatment depends largely on the degree of attention given, and obtained. Consequently, it is well to get the patient quieted down, before beginning the actual treatment. The healer may talk to him in a quiet low tone of voice, bidding the patient relax every muscle and take the tension from every nerve. He should adapt the conversation to the individual requirements of the patient, speaking only of those things calculated to promote quietness and calmness of mind, and to carefully avoid subjects likely to arouse antagonism and argument. Remember, you are not there to convert the patient to any particular belief of yours—you are to *cure* him. Let your manner and conversation be Soothing and Quieting.

Voice

The Healer should pay much attention to cultivating a good "Suggestive Voice." It is difficult to describe just what is meant by this term, but a few words of explanation may be of value. We do not mean that the Healer should endeavor to become a skilled elocutionist, but we do mean that he should be able to throw feeling and earnestness into his tone. He should endeavor to have his Thought and Desire so permeate his tone that the vibrations may be felt by the patient. His tone should be Vibrant and Strong not necessarily loud, but possessed of that peculiar quality that we call Strength. The words should fairly vibrate, and penetrate into the mind of the patient. A mental state of forgetting one's self, and concentrating the whole mind on the meaning of the words used will produce the result practice, of course, improving the gift and faculty. The tone should be "tense."

The following exercises will aid the Suggestor:

Imagine yourself as treating a patient by Suggestion. Imagine the patient as sitting in a chair in front of you, or else, reclining on a couch with yon standing or sitting by his side. Then give him the suggestions applicable to his case, telling him just what result to expect to accomplish, and telling him firmly and positively that the result WILL be accomplished. Pick out the key-words of the suggestion that is the strong, vibrant words that you wish to stand out in his mind during and after the treatment, and practice repeating them until you feel that they are vibrant and intense, with the real meaning and intent.

Take the word "STRONG" for instance since it is a word that should be used frequently in suggestive treatment. Repeat the word several times, increasing the intensity and earnestness at each repetition, thus Strong; Strong; STRONG; STRONG. Practice until yon can fairly feel the vibration of the word throughout your entire being until the word actually objectifies the Thought behind it. Then take the word "WELL," and practice on it in the same way. You must not repeat the words like a recorder, or parrot, but must endeavor to FEEL what you are saying.

Practice this frequently, and you will begin to find that you will acquire a Vibrant Suggestive tone, that will make your words ring with intensity, and cause them to be felt by the patient. Let the two words, Earnestness and Intensity be ever before you in acquiring the Suggestive Voice.

The Eye

The Suggestionist should cultivate a firm, earnest gaze of the eye. Not a stare, but a firm powerful gaze. This may be acquired by gradual practice and thought. A person always gazes earnestly at a thing that holds his attention, so if you will train yourself to look with interest and attention, you will find that the proper gaze will come to you without any further special attention. We advise the cultivation of this gaze, not with the idea of any hypnotic influence, or anything of that sort, but with the idea of concentrating the thought, and holding the attention of the patient. Besides this, it is calculated to create confidence in the mind of the patient who feels more or less uncertain and who lacks confidence. And without confidence on the part of the patient, healing by any method or system is rendered more difficult, since in such cases the patient pulls against the healer instead of with him.

The Mental Attitude of the Healer

The Suggestive Healer should cultivate a Mental Attitude of Earnestness. He should not be a trifler. He should have the best interests of the patient at heart, and in so doing his own best interests will be served.

He should act with a purpose, and not scatter his efforts and life in petty non-essentials. We do not mean to indicate that the healer should follow a life of all work and no play—quite the contrary, for we believe that Work, Play, and Rest, are equal necessities to the normal man. We do mean, however, that he should see his purpose, and move accordingly.

He should be Concentrated in his work. A wandering attention and lack of concentration is fatal to good suggestive work. Not only do the suggestions fail to have the proper effect, but the patient subtly feels that something is lacking, and he does not receive the proper vibrations. Use the Will and hold the Mind down to its work.

He should have confidence in himself, and if this be lacking he should build up that confidence by a practice of Auto-suggestion or affirmation. Because, unless one have confidence in himself, he cannot expect others to have it. Confidence is contagious, and so is lack of it. Remember that.

Position of the Patient

The patient should be placed in an easy, comfortable position. A reclining, or Morris chair, or a conch, is the best thing to use in bringing about the easy condition of physical comfort. The patient should be taught to relax his muscles, the best way to teach same being to ask the patient to allow his hand to be "limp," and then raising it, the healer should allow it to drop of its own weight to the chair, telling the patient to allow an equally relaxed condition to prevail all over the body. Use the suggestion: "Now make yourself perfectly comfortable easy, easy, easy, easy and comfortable easy and comfortable," the suggestion acting not only to cause the physical ease and relaxation, but also the mental relaxation and withdrawal of tension from the nerves. The healer should either sit beside the patient on a low stool, or else stand by his side, or back of him. Use your own intuition in these matters, as there are no invariable rules necessary to be observed.

Repetition

One of the axioms of Suggestive Therapeutics is that "Suggestions gain increased force by repetition." A constant repetition of the suggestions fastens it firmly upon the mind of the patient, therefore the healer should repeat the key word of the suggestion again and again not so as to become monotonous but in a different arrangement of words, remembering to bring the key word, or principal suggestion into each new arrangement. Remember that planting a suggestion is like attacking a fort. It must be attacked from all sides, and so a repetition of the suggestion in different forms is important. In repeating the suggestion, let the key word ring out strong and vibrant.

Surroundings

The treatment should be given, so far as is possible, amidst surroundings that do not tend to distract the patient's attention from the suggestions. Endeavor to shut out all outside noises and sights, so that the sense of hearing of the patient may be focused and concentrated on the suggestions that are being given him or her. Pull down the blinds of the room, so as to produce a state of semi-darkness or dusk. These things have a great psychological importance.

Picturing the Expected Condition

In giving the suggestions, it is important to picture in the mind of the patient, the desired condition that is the condition that you wish to bring about. Lead him up to it by degrees, picturing each, process of the expected cure, and winding up with a mental picture of him restored to health. In the General Treatment given a little later on, you will see just what we mean. We mention it here that you may understand why the picture is given. Thought takes form in action, and the mind of the patient closely following the picture, in treatment after treatment, unconsciously causes the physical to manifest the suggested thought-picture.

General Remarks

There is no special magic in the words uttered by the suggestionist, and the whole virtue of the suggestive treatment lies in the *Thought behind the words*. To the degree that this thought is taken and absorbed by the patient, is the degree of the success of the treatment. Therefore it follows that the degree of success lies in the degree of Energy and Earnestness that the healer puts into Ms thought, and the degree of Earnestness and Energy whereby the thought is conveyed by the words and otherwise from healer to patient. Of course there is a constant mental or telepathic transmission of the Thought, but the effect is heightened by the strong suggestive words of the healer, and the combination of the two is a powerful one. The patient's mind should be constantly directed to *the conditions expected and hoped to be realized*.

IMPORTANT RULE

Never make any reference to the diseased condition

during your suggestions, but always speak of the condition as you wish it to be. Lead the mind away from the present condition, and place it on the expected condition. You thereby place an ideal in the mind of the patient, which he will, unconsciously, endeavor to live up to.

Do not neglect to observe the above rule, for it is most important. Make no negative suggestions or "denials," but always make positive suggestions or "affirmations." For instance, do not suggest: "You are not weak, etc.", but on the contrary suggest, repeatedly, "You are Strong." Do you see the difference? The reason lies in the fact that by repeating the word of the thing you would deny, you really affirm its existence, and direct the mind of the patient to it

CHAPTER XIV

SUGGESTIVE TREATMENTS

In giving Suggestive treatments, the healer should always carry in his mind a mental picture of the conditions that he wishes to bring about. This mental picture will enable him to give the proper suggestions easily, and instinctively, besides giving the patient of the effect of the projected thought, according to the lines of Thought-transference, which last phase of the subject will be touched upon in the chapters treating on Mental Healing.

The healer should acquaint himself with the conditions which he wishes to bring about (and which will be described in this chapter) and then proceed to suggest closely on those lines.

It is always well to begin the first treatment by a little conversation to the patient concerning the power of the mind over the body, and the wonderful effect that mental suggestions have over the affected parts. Be careful and do not get into theory or complicated details, for remember that the patient has not advanced as far in the subject as have you, and theory and details will only confuse him. Stick to the "effects" to be produced, and content yourself with speaking of the power of mind over the bodily organs, etc., without launching long theories of the various planes of mind, etc. Let the patient know what you expect to do, and accomplish, and so far as possible get him to cooperate with you by forming a mental picture as you suggest to him.

You will notice that in the general treatment that we give here, we have, included suggestions that give the patient an additional idea of the power of the mind. It is well to do this occasionally, in order to keep up the interest in the treatment, which is highly important, for the degree of interest is often the degree of receptivity to the treatment.

In giving treatment, do not strive to repeat the exact words of our general treatments get the idea and give it in your own words. Your own words will mean more to you, and you will be able to enter into the spirit of the thing better than by merely repeating the words of others.

The following is a fair General Treatment:

GENERAL SUGGESTIVE TREATMENT

After getting the patient to relax and place himself in a quiet, easy, restful position, say to him:

"Now, Mr. X (or Mrs. X, as the case may be) you are resting easy, quiet and composed. Your body is at rest—every muscle is relaxed—every nerve is at rest. You are feeling quiet, calm, and restful, all over, from head to foot, from head to foot. Quiet, restful, and easy. Your mind is calm and composed, and you will let my healing suggestions sink deep, deep, down in your subconscious mind, that they may manifest health and strength for you. Like a seed that is planted in good soil, they will grow and bear good fruit of health, and strength for you."

"I shall begin by strengthening your stomach and organs of nutrition, for from those organs you obtain the nourishment which will build you up, and give you new strength. I will cause your stomach to digest the proper amount of food, and then assimilate it, and convert it into nourishment that will be carried to all parts of your body, building up and strengthening cells, parts and organs. You need perfect nourishment, and I am going to cause your organs of nutrition to give it to you.

"Your stomach is strong, strong, strong—strong and able and willing and ready to do good work for you, and to digest the food needed for your nourishment. It will begin today—right now—to manifest strength and power, so that it will digest your food and properly nourish you. You must get the proper nourishment in order to be well, and therefore we begin right here at the stomach. Your stomach is strong, strong, strong and well, and ready to begin its work. You will begin to feel this increase of strength in the stomach—you are beginning to feel it now, and you will find that day by day it will become stronger and stronger and will do its work better and better each day. Your stomach and organs of nutrition are ready to do their work properly, and will begin to send nourishment to all parts of the body—and that is what you need—that is what you need. I can send impulses to those tired organs, and giving them new strength and health and power, and you will be conscious of the improvement at once. Remember, now, nourishment, nourishment, nourishment—that is what we are after for you, and that is what we will get right now—right from the beginning.

"And I expect yon to cooperate with me and try to think bright, happy and cheerful thoughts all the time, all the time. Bright, cheerful and happy thoughts will drive away the diseased conditions—

will drive them away, I say. Think bright, cheerful and happy thoughts, and you will find a decided improvement in your mental and physical states. Remember, now, bright, cheerful and happy—commit the words to memory and repeat them often.

"Now, we are going to equalize your circulation. Next to nutrition, the circulation is the important thing. You will begin right now to manifest an equal and proper circulation all over your body, from head to foot—from head to foot. The blood will course freely and easily through your entire body—from head to foot carrying with it nourishment and strength to every part. It will return carrying with it the waste matter of the cells, and organs, and parts, which will be burnt up in the lungs and expelled from the body, being replaced by the fresh good material in the blood. Now breathe deeply several times and burn up the waste diseased matter that the blood is carrying back with it to be burnt up by the oxygen in the lungs which you have breathed into it. You are breathing in health and strength—health and strength, I say, and you will feel better from now on. Practice deep breathing occasionally and think that you are drawing in health and strength and breathing out the old diseased conditions. For that is just what you are doing; perfect circulation all over the body and proper breathing to assist in the good work.

"You must begin, also, to get rid of the waste products of the system by drinking the proper amount of water each day. You must increase your supply of fluids. You must have a glass of water near and you must occasionally take a sip or so from it, saying 'I am taking this water to cleanse my system from impurities, and to bring about new, normal and healthy conditions.' Do not neglect this because it is most important. A plant needs water in order to be healthy, and so do you. So do not neglect the water.

"Your increased fluid supply will cause your bowels to move regularly every day and thus carry off the waste matter of the system. Your bowels will begin tomorrow morning to move naturally and easily, and you will soon get into a regular habit. You must assist me in this work by holding the thought occasionally that your bowels will begin to move naturally.

"Now we have begun the good work, and you must keep it up. You will begin to get nourishment from your food, by reason of the improvement in your organs of nutrition. Every part of you is being strengthened, and day by day you will note an improvement. Your circulation will be equalized and your general system will be benefited thereby. You will breathe freely, and thus strengthen the body and also burn up the old waste materials. You will get rid of the old waste matter by taking additional fluids, as I have said, and your bowels moving properly will rid your system of the poisonous debris of the system. You will be bright, cheerful and happy, strong and well.

"You are stronger all over, from head to foot from head to foot and every organ, cell and part is functioning properly now, and health, and strength, and energy, and vigor are coming to you coming to you right now.

Then give specific suggestions regarding the particular parts that seem to be giving the trouble the suggestions being modeled along the lines of what you want. Suggest that the pain will leave, and that normal conditions will begin to reassert themselves.

You will find that the General Treatment given above will work a great improvement in those treated by it, irrespective of the local nature of their trouble. Their secret is that if you manage to restore proper and normal conditions of nutrition, assimilation and elimination, the rest takes care of itself. A man or woman with perfect digestion, assimilation and elimination—that is with proper nutrition and proper clearing away of the "Ashes of the System," can not help but be a well person. We urge you to carefully read our book "Hatha Yoga" and acquaint yourselves with the importance of these things. You may "work in" the teachings of "Hatha Yoga" in your suggestions and the advice thus given will be of the greatest value and importance to the patient.

Acquaint yourself with the rules of right living, as given in our book "Hatha Yoga" and you will have the secret of health in your own hands. By suggesting these things to patients you will fix the ideas in their minds by suggestion, and change their habits of living from imperfect to perfect, so that when you get them well they will stay well. Suggestion along these lines will prove a God-send to the people you treat, if you, will but fix the idea firmly in your own mind, so that you may be able to pass it on to them in the same way.

You will find that imperfect nutrition and constipation are the principal things to be overcome, no matter what is the nature of the complaint. Explain this to your patient and tell him that by suggestion you will restore the normal conditions, which you will be able to do.

In cases of female troubles, such as imperfect menstruation, etc., the above treatment will work wonders. Give the suggestions of regular menstruation, just as you gave the suggestion of normal action of the bowels the principle is the same. Tell the patient to look forward to the time for the regular menstrual period, with confidence, and let her fix her mind on the date some time ahead. In a month or so regular habits will be restored in many cases.

It is not necessary for us to go into detail about the treatment of various complaints by suggestion. We have given you the master key and you can readily adapt the treatment to all kinds of troubles. Remember always, however, to insist upon proper nutrition and elimination and equalized circulation with breathing, for these things constitute a universal panacea. Bead over the other forms of psychic healing mentioned in this book. You will get a little something from each of them.

CHAPTER XV

SELF-SUGGESTION

"As a man thinketh in his heart so is he," is an old saying the truth of which becomes more and more apparent to us each year. In the chapter in which we showed the effect of the mind on the body you will notice that the majority of the physical troubles brought about by thought-influence were brought about by the thought of the person themselves by self-suggestion, so to speak. A man's physical health is largely a matter of his self-suggestion. If he maintains a mental attitude of health, strength and fearlessness, he manifests accordingly. And if he goes about with a mind filled with ideas and thoughts of a depressing nature his body will likewise respond.

Fear is the great cause of disease. Fear acts as a poison on the physical system, and its effects are manifest in many directions. Remove fear and you have removed the cause of the trouble, and the symptoms will gradually disappear.

But all this we have stated elsewhere—and this book must be a *book of practice*, rather than of theory. The question is how person may treat himself, or herself, by self-suggestion.

The answer is quite simple—it is that the person may give himself just the suggestions that he would give a patient, following the advice and instructions given in the last chapter. The "I" part of you may give suggestions to that part of the mind that runs the physical organism and manages the body from cell to organ. These suggestions will be taken and acted upon if given with sufficient earnestness. Just as people may make themselves sick by improper self-suggestions, so may they restore themselves to health by the proper suggestions given in the same manner.

There is no mystery about this—it is in accordance with a well established psychological law.

The best way for you to start in a course of self-suggestion for yourself, presuming that you need the same, is to read carefully our book "Hatha Yoga" which contains practical instruction and information about "Right Living." Then after having acquired this plan of right living start in to practice right thinking. Right thinking consists in maintaining the proper mental attitude of cheerfulness and fearlessness. These two things are a battery of force.

If you have imperfect health rest assured that it is caused by the violation of some natural law. You may discover what this violated natural law is by reference to "Hatha Yoga," and then it becomes your duty to correct the habit and restore natural functioning by self-suggestions or right thinking.

In nine cases out of ten you will find that the root of the trouble lies in improper nutrition and imperfect elimination. You don't believe this, you say ! Well, then, let us tell you your symptoms and see if they do not come out about right to fit your case.

First, you have a poor appetite and imperfect digestion dyspepsia or indigestion. Then you are constipated, and if a woman yon have scanty and irregular menstruation. Then your hands and feet are cold, denoting imperfect circulation. Then your eyesight and hearing is affected—you have ringing in the ears and cloudy vision. Your taste is affected—your smell is also poor and you are liable to have symptoms of catarrh. But your sense of feeling is not poor—it is abnormally sensitive, and you are called "nervous." You do not get a good night's sleep and you feel used up all the time. Your skin is colorless and your cheeks pale. Your lips and finger nails lack the rosy color of health. And so on.

Now does this not fit your case? Isn't it queer how we have diagnosed your complaint without having ever seen you, or known of you? But this is no miracle, we assure you we have merely recited the symptoms arising from what may be called a typical case of malnutrition and imperfect elimination. And the cause of these symptoms lies in the two things named. Then the removal of the cause lies in a correction of bad habits of living and bad habits of thinking. And "Hatha Yoga" will give you the habits of right living, and self-suggestion will aid you in right thinking and the speedy removal of the trouble

Treat yourself According to the lines of the General Treatment given under the head of Suggestive Treatments in the last chapter. Make the treatments vigorous just as earnest as if you were treating somebody else instead of yourself. And you will get wonderful results.

See yourself in your "mind's eye" as you wish, yourself to be. Then start in to think of yourself as being that, and then live as the healthy man or woman should do. Then talk up to yourself and tell your instinctive mind what you expect it to do for you and insist on it taking hold of the physical body and building up new cells and tissue and discarding the old worn out and diseased material. And it will obey you like a well trained assistant or helper and you will begin to manifest health and strength.

There is no special mystery about this self-suggestion. It is merely your "I" telling your instinctive mind to get to work and attend to its affairs properly. And by right living you give the instinctive mind the material with which to work and the conditions conducive to success.

We could fill page after page of this book with "Suggestions" and "Affirmations" for you to use in different complaints. But this is useless. You can make up your own suggestions and affirmations, which will answer just as well as would ours. Just speak up to the instinctive mind just as if it were another person who had charge of your body and tell it what you expect it to do. Do not hesitate about being in earnest about it—put some life into your commands. Talk to it in earnest. Say to it "Here, you instinctive mind, I want you to get down to work and manage things better for me. I am tired of this old trouble and intend to get rid of it. I am eating nourishing food, and my stomach is strong enough to digest it properly, and I insist on your attending to it right away, now. I am drinking sufficient water to carry off the waste matter from the system and I insist on your seeing that my bowels move regularly every day. I insist on your seeing that my circulation is equalized and made normal. I am breathing properly and burning up the waste matter and properly oxygenizing the blood and you must do the rest Get to work—get to work." Add to this any instructions that you think well and then see how the instinctive mind will "get down to business." See what we have said on this subject in the chapter on "Thought-Force Healing." Then maintain the proper mental attitude, bracing yourself with strong affirmations until you get things going right. Say to yourself "I am getting strong and well—I am manifesting health," etc., etc. Now we have told you how to do it then GET TO WOEK AND DO IT!

CHAPTER XVI

MENTAL HEALING

The reader will see by reference to the chapter on Suggestive Healing the effect on the physical body by incorrect thinking, and it is not deemed necessary to repeat those illustrations or examples here, nor to give additional ones. It is presumed that every reader of this book has some acquaintance with the effect of mental states on physical functioning, so it is not necessary to take up space with further proofs of the same.

The theory and system of mental healing is based on this knowledge of the effect of mind on body, coupled with the idea that as the mind may produce abnormal functioning, so may the process be reversed and used to restore perfect health and correct functioning. We shall not attempt to recite the special theories of the several schools of mental healing, nor to attempt to explain the many theories regarding the question of "What is Mind?" nor the psychological theories regarding the process of the cures. The fact is that mental healing is a fact—and the thing to do is to tell how to make use of and apply it.

In our chapters on Suggestive Healing we have given information that may well be combined with these teachings regarding mental healing. In fact, suggestion and mental healing are twins—each representing one side of the same thing. The principal difference rests in the manner of applying the force behind the treatment. Suggestion depends almost altogether on verbal suggestions, etc., while Mental Healing depends on telepathy or thought-transmission. The best healers combine both methods when the patient is in their presence. But mental healing does not require the presence of the patient, the treatments often being given to patients many miles away by what is known as "Absent Treatment," but which is really a form of telepathy.

Telepathy, once laughed at as a superstitious fancy, is now beginning to be recognized by the scientific world, and will soon be adopted as a law. It has been known to occultists in all ages and times, among all people and it is not a "new" thing by any means, although many claim to have "discovered" it in our own times.

We give a few examples of its general acceptance among men of intelligence and prominence in our own times.

Edw. T. Bennett, late secretary of the Society of Psychical Research, says: "The conclusion seems to be irresistible that the five senses do not exhaust the means by which knowledge may enter the mind. In other words, the investigator seems to be driven to the conscious that thought-transference or telepathy must now be included among scientifically proven facts"

Prof. John D. Quackenbos, the eminent New York scientist, says: "The time has indeed come, as Maeterlinck predicted it would, when souls may know of each other without the intermediary of the senses."

Clark Bell says: "Telepathy, as it is regarded by scientists who accept it as a fact, is some unknown sense of power of the human body, by which as a physical process communication is held between brain and brain or the human organism—some means by which the perceptions are reached in some manner analogous to the known and well defined transmission of the electric current, or the action of gravitation which we know exists. But we are as yet unable to comprehend how it acts, or to know its methods. "

Prof. Crookes, the well known English scientist, says: "If we accept the theory that the brain is composed of separate elements—nerve cells—then we must presume that each of these components, like every other bit of matter, has its movements of vibration, and will, under suitable conditions, be affected; as for instance, the nerve cells of the retina by vibration in the ether. If another neuron, situated not far away, should acquire the same movement of vibration, there seems to be no good reason why they should not materially affect each other through the ether."

Dr. Sheldon Leavitt says: "There is no disputing the fact that those who have given the subject of telepathy attentive thought and patient investigation have become convinced of its truth and practicability. My own experience has given me unwavering convictions. I know that in some way thought can be transmitted from one conscious mind to another; and I have good reason to believe that it can be transmitted still more forcibly and fully to the unconscious mind of the recipient. "

Camille Flammarion, the French astronomer, says: "We sum up, therefore, our preceding observations by the conclusion that one mind can act on another at a distance without the habitual medium of words, or any other visible means of communication. It appears to us altogether unreasonable to reject this conclusion if we accept the facts. There is nothing unscientific, nothing romantic in admitting that an idea can influence a brain from a distance. The action of one human being on another, from a distance, is a scientific fact; it is as certain as the existence of Paris, of Napoleon, of Oxygen, or of Sirius." Again the same authority says: "There can be no doubt that our psychical force creates a movement of the ether, which transmits itself afar like all movements of ether, and re-becomes perceptible to brains in harmony with our own. The transformation of a psychic adverse, may be analogous to what takes place on a telephone, where the receptive plate, which is identical with the plate at the other end, reconstructs the sonorous movement transmitted, not by means of sound, but by electricity. But these are only comparisons. "

Page after page could be filled with like expressions of belief in thought-transmission, on the part of the thinking public, but the same is not deemed necessary. Those who wish further information on this subject are referred to the published reports of the English Society for Psychical Research, which may be found in the main libraries of the country.

It is by means of this fact of telepathy that the "absent healing" of the Mental Scientists; and others are performed when they are not occasioned by direct verbal suggestion, which factor must not be overlooked.

The principle of mental healing lies in the fact that the central mind controls the bodily functions—or the mind manifesting through the organs, cells and parts of the body. The latter respond to the mental states of the central mind and anything affecting the latter naturally affects the former. The healer endeavors to establish in the central mind of the patient a normal condition of mental attitude. This normal mental attitude is one in which the individual recognizes his mastery of the body, and of his entire system. This mental attitude when once acquired will prevent disease and will restore health when disease has once set in. Its healing power depends on the degree of realization of the supremacy of mind manifested by the person.

Now this realization is imperfect in the average sick person who has allowed himself to sink gradually down to the lower planes of the mind and has allowed his realization to become impaired from some one or more of various cause. Here is where the healer comes into use and service. He has kept his mind positive and keen, and has trained himself in the science of thought-transmission. Therefore when called on to treat a patient he raises his "vibration" until they reach the proper stage, when he transmits them to the mind of patient, the result being that the vibrations are reproduced there, and the consequence is that the mind of the patient reacts on the mind principal animating the parts, organs and cells—the instinctive mind, in fact, and gradually reestablishes normal conditions.

The various schools of mental healing have a variety of theories to account for their healings, but we think that the above will be found to cover all the general ideas and theories—and in fact, to account for what happens, irrespective of metaphysical theories, and in spite of some of them. There is a natural law underlying all these forms of healing and it is folly to attempt to befog the facts with a mass of metaphysical theorizing. The fact is that all the schools make cures, and perform healing, in spite of their conflicting theories. Does not this prove that they are all using the same force and power in spite of their theories? "We shall not attempt to take up these various theories in detail, but shall at once proceed to the "proof of the pudding" by giving you in the next chapter a plain system of Practice of Mental Healing, which will enable any of you to perform the healing work accomplished by the various schools.

CHAPTER XVII

MENTAL HEALING METHODS

The student is advised to acquaint himself thoroughly with what we have written on the questions of thought-force treatments, suggestive treatments, metaphysical treatments, etc., in order to get a full *general idea* of what is required to be held in the mind of the healer in giving treatments. He may take such parts of each as appeal to him, leaving the others for those to whom they appeal. Let the intuition decide this matter for each of you— it will act for your best interests and success in healing.

In giving mental healing treatments, the mind of the healer must be able to picture the desired conditions in the patient—that is to mentally see the patient as healed, and the parts, organs and cells functioning normally. In short, in the degree that the healer is able to mentally visualize the normal conditions, so will be the degree of success in mental healing.

Dismiss all doubt from your mind, and train your mind to *see* the desired condition just as if it were actually before you, exposed to your physical gaze. Train yourself in this from day to day and you will be surprised to see how rapidly you advance until you attain the sense of power and healing that will sweep over you like a wave.

So far as transmitting the thought is concerned, that requires no strenuous effort on the part of the healer. The main difficulty lies in the ability to form the mental image, just described—that once formed the thought is easily transmitted by *merely thinking of it as occurring.*

This last may seem strange to many of you who have understood, or have been taught, that great concentration and effort were needed in order to project a thought. This teaching is incorrect, the truth being that the concentration is needed only for the purpose of producing a clear cut mental image— clear visualizing—and that once accomplished the transmission or projection is accomplished by a mere act of desire or will, in other words, *in thinking of it as occurring.* Some healers and adepts in thought transmission have found it of advantage to them in their work to *imagine* that they could see the thought *actually leave* their brain; *actually travel* through space; and *actually be received* by the mind of the patient. This plan certainly will aid the mind in holding firm to the mental image until it takes effect.

In treating a patient who is present you should first tell him to quiet and calm himself—in short, you should endeavor to get him to go into the Silence as much as possible. We do not mean by this that he should go to sleep, or slumber, but merely that he should calm his mind, and withdraw his thoughts from the things and scenes of the outer life, so far as is possible. In order to aid in bringing about this effect, you should endeavor to have the room made quiet and still, and should also avoid bright lights which are apt to distract the attention.

With the proper condition once established you should sit quietly until you feel that your own mental state is right for the treatment—that your vibrations are raised to the proper degree (your own feelings must decide this for you), then you may begin the treatment proper. From a mental image of the patient restored to health—form a mental ideal of the proper conditions and then "think" of that condition transferred to the mind of the patient—a transferral of the mental photograph as it were. You may use words in forming the mental conditions you wish—silently, of course. The main thing is to form the mental picture of the ideal condition that you wish to bring about. Remember this always. Try to mentally visualize your patient as restored to perfect health and endeavor to hold that picture constantly before the mind during the treatment.

It may be well to supplement the treatment by words of advice and encouragement for the patient, and a little instruction in the power of his own mind in the direction of co-operation with your thought.

In "absent treatment, or distant healing" as it is called, the healer should proceed in exactly the same way as if the patient were present. He should imagine that the patient is right in the room before him and then he should address the treatment just as if he were addressing it to the patient in person. The thoughts should be "seen" mentally to leave, travel and reach the patient. Many healers in giving absent treatment speak mentally to the patient (as if he were present) telling him the things that should be told him, just as if he were present in person to hear them. This "distant talk" may consist merely of suggestions of health, strength and restored vitality, or, on the other hand, of "statements" of truth and being, such as are used by the metaphysical healers. It should be unnecessary to add that the healing thought of Love is a most powerful aid to the restoration of Health. Let your thought of Love sweep through the mind of the patient, driving out all adverse and negative thoughts that have been lodging there.

In giving absent treatments it will be helpful if the

patient will place himself in a quiet, receptive attitude during the time of treatment, this result being accomplished by yourself and the patient agreeing upon the hour or time of treatment. However, this is not imperative or absolutely essential, as many healers do not treat their patients at any particular time, but give the treatment when the conditions seem best to them.

Now, any attempt to give fuller and more detailed instructions in the matter of giving this form of treatment would be useless, and mere repetition. We have given you in a few words the master key to the treatment—the very essence of the teachings. If you will impress these instructions upon your mind, in connection with what we have given you under the head of Suggestive Treatments, Thought-Force Treatments and Absent Pranic Treatments, you will be able to give most powerful and effective mental treatments. We might make a book out of this one phase of the subject alone, by merely padding out the subject and repeating what we have already told you in other parts of the book. But this is unnecessary and foreign to the purpose of this book, which aims to be a simple, plain, concise teacher of the methods of psychic healing in its various forms.

The book must be read, studied and considered as a whole, for the instructions given in one method have a bearing on those given under another head. To give full detailed instructions under each head would make three or four books instead of one. So kindly remember that you should acquaint yourselves with, all of the methods given in order to obtain the full benefit of the instructions imparted.

CHAPTER XVIII

METAPHYSICAL HEALING

The term which is used as a title for this chapter is a much abused one, and is employed by different people to describe nearly all forms of healing mentioned in this book

Of course, everyone using any form of psychic healing has a certain right to call his healing "Metaphysical," for the word metaphysical means "beyond the physical," but the generally accepted sense of the term "Metaphysics" means "The Science of Being." And according to strict interpretation of the term metaphysical healing should be applied only to that form of healing arising only from the actual realization on the part of the patient of the reality behind appearances—of real being—of the real self of the universe. To one who is able to unfold into an actual realization of that which-is, there is at his disposal a wonderful healing power, both for himself and others, if he knows how to apply the same. But this knowledge is not always evidenced by those who unfold into the higher consciousness, and, in fact, there is a decided tendency on the part of some of these people to neglect the physical altogether as unworthy of thought, the attention being turned entirely on the higher planes of being. This position is wrong, for the physical plays a needed part in the unfoldment of the Ego, and to neglect it is to run contrary to the law of life.

The actual process of this form of metaphysical healing may be spoken of as a control of the lower by the power coming from the higher consciousness. The higher consciousness so manifests its power that it controls the lower. But, after all, it would appear that the real cause of the cure actually is found in the fact that the mind, being occupied in a contemplation of its higher planes of manifestation, ceases to concern itself with the workings of the lower planes, and consequently the latter operates according to the well established laws of the universe without interference, and without the constant injection of negative thought which produces abnormal conditions in so many people.

A realization of the higher nature and being of one, has a tendency to uplift one above the thoughts of fear and worry, which act as poisons and cause disease in so many people. And, the interference of fear thought being removed nature (or what stands behind the word) operates freely and without hindrance.

We shall describe higher phases of metaphysical healing in the next two chapters, under the term "Spiritual Healing," which we consider more appropriate.

In this chapter we refer principally to the forms of healing used by some of the metaphysical healers who confine their healing process to teaching the patient certain metaphysical systems, containing a greater or lesser degree of truth.

But, even in these last mentioned forms of treatment, you will see that unconsciously the healer must be calling into effect the power of mental healing or suggestion, or both. The "treatment" that always follows the metaphysical talk, must call into operation mental healing, or suggestion, although the healer may not know it, and may indignantly repudiate this fact, and state that the treatment given is "something entirely different." But, nevertheless, the student of psychic healing may readily recognize mental healing and suggestion under the many disguises draped around it. The best proof of the fact that there is a common principle operated, may be found in the fact that the different schools of metaphysical healing, so called, work cures, in about the same proportion in spite of their various theories and creeds. Of course they all have a common ground of agreement in their belief in the One Life and Spirit, but they vehemently oppose each others claims, and call each other "victims of error," and other pleasant names but still all go on making cures, and doing good healing work, nevertheless. Christian Science, and Anti-Christian Science schools and cults, seem to do equally good healing work. All this would seem to indicate that some one healing force is used by all, and that no sect has any monopoly of it.

The Power of the One Life is Always There—always ready and willing to be used by those who demand and use it, irrespective of the particular beliefs and theories or creeds of those using it. Like the sunshine and the rain it falls upon all alike, who expose themselves to its power, or who attract it to them. It is All for All. The petty theories and differences of the cults are most amusing when one considers the Infinite One. What children in spiritual knowledge even the best of us are—each claiming that he has the only truth, and the whole truth, and that all the others are in "error." The truth seems to be that ALL have the Truth, or portions of it fitting into their understandings. And that NONE have ALL the Truth.

The Love and Power of the Infinite is equally the

right of the individual seeker after the Truth, as of the cult or sect that claims to be the mouthpiece of the All. Creeds are born, rise, fall and die—cults and sects and schools pursue the same Path. All is birth, growth and death—relatively, of course—all obey the Law, which may be called Evolution. Ages, people, races, lands, schools, cults, creeds, sects, leaders, may come and go—*must* come and go—but the Law ever remains, unchangeable, unerring, unvarying, deathless, endless. Over all the Law reigns—all do its bidding. None are its sole agents and mouthpieces—and yet All are its agents and mouthpieces. It uses all—and yet is used by All. When this mystery is understood, then there is peace.

It is useless to attempt to teach Metaphysical Healing to those who do not at least partially understand the higher teaching. To those who wish, to know more regarding these teachings, we would recommend the "*Advanced Course in Yogi Philosophy*," published by the same people who publish this little book. To those who understand and who wish to heal themselves and others by this method, we would say that the only rule is this:

Go into the Silence and meditate on the Real Self. When the Realization comes, then give the healing treatment to yourself or others in some appropriate words, conveying the thought so far as may be (it is impossible to convey it fully in words). The following form will answer if you cannot frame one yourself:

TREATMENT

Oh, Spirit—the One, Birthless, Deathless—Omniscient, Omnipresent, Omnipotent in whose Ocean of Life I am a drop—let me feel thy Presence and Power. Let me realize even more fully what Thou art, and what I am in Thee. Let the consciousness of Thy Reality, and My Reality in Spirit, permeate my being, and descend upon all the planes of my mind. Let the Power of Spirit manifest through my mind permeating the body of this other Self that I am desirous of healing (or "this body that I call mine own") bringing to it Health, and Strength, and Life, that it may be rendered a more fitting Temple of the Spirit—a more perfect instrument of Expression for the One Life that flows through it. Raise up this body from the gross vibrations of the lower planes, to the higher vibrations of the Spiritual Mind, through which we know Thee. Give this body, through the Mind that animates it, that Peace, Strength, and Life, that is its by virtue of its being. Do Thou, the All-Life, flow in thy essence through this the Part, re-vivifying and enlivening it. This do I claim, O, All-Spirit, by virtue of my eternal Birthright from Thee. And by reason of Thy promise and inner knowledge given to me, I now demand it of Thee."

In place of this, or in connection with this, you may use any of the many "Statements of Being" that the various "Science" bodies use—for they are all good. But remember this always there is no magic in mere words—and no cult has any proprietary right to any special words. The words are free to you, and to all—and the virtue thereof lies in the thought and realization back of the words, Words come, go and change, but Thought and Realization which express them is Eternal. Read the next two chapters in connection with this one.

CHAPTER XIX

SPIRITUAL HEALING

This is the highest form of healing, and is much rarer and less common than is generally believed to be the case. Many healers doing very good work along the lines of Mental Healing, believe, and teach, that their work is done along Spiritual lines. But in this they are mistaken. True Spiritual Healing is not "done" by anyone. In such cases the healer becomes an instrument or channel through which flows the Spiritual Healing Force of the Universe. That is, the healer is able to open up his Spiritual Mind as a channel for the inflow of the Spiritual force of the Universe, which passes through the Healer into the Spiritual Mind of the patient, and there sets up vibrations of such intensity and strength that it invigorates the lower Mental Principles, and finally the organs and parts themselves, restoring them to normal condition. Spiritual cures are often practically *instantaneous*, although it does not necessarily follow that they must always be so.

The Spiritual Healer allowing the Spiritual Healing Force to flow through him to the patient, causes the latter to be literally "bathed in a flow of Spirit," as we have heard it expressed.

In order to understand this form of treatment, intelligently, the reader must acquaint himself with the Yogi teachings regarding the several Mental Principles, which teaching he will find in the "*Lessons in Yogi Philosophy and Eastern Mysticism,*" published by the same publishers as this book. We do not care to repeat here what we have said on this subject, although it may be well to say a few words regarding the Spiritual Mind, that this form of treatment may be better understood.

The Spiritual Mind of man is that principle of mind that is above and higher than the two lower mental principles known as Instinctive Mind and Intellect, respectively. Spiritual Mind is *above* the plane of Intellect, just as the Instinctive Mind is *below* the plane of Intellect. The Spiritual Mind has not as yet developed or unfolded into consciousness in the average man, although some of the more advanced of the human race—those who have gone ahead of their brothers on The Path—have unfolded the

Spiritual Mind into consciousness, or, rather, have moved the centre of consciousness into the region of the Spiritual Mind. This higher Mental Principle is what we try to express when we say the "Something Within" that seems to exert a protecting influence over us, and which sends us words of caution or advice in moments of need.

All that the human race has received in the way of noble, elevating, higher thoughts have come from this region of the mind. The Spiritual Mind projects fragments of truth into the lower Mental Principals. All that has come to the human race, in its evolution, that has tended toward nobility, true religious feeling, kindness, humanity, justice, unselfish love, mercy, sympathy, etc., has come to it through the slowly unfolding Spiritual Mind. As the unfoldment goes on, man's idea of Justice increases, and he has more compassion. His feeling of Human, Brotherhood increases—his idea of love grows, and he increases in all the qualities which men of all creeds pronounce "good."

The Spiritual Mind is the source of the "inspiration" which certain poets, painters, sculptors, writers, preachers, orators, and others have received in all times, and which they receive today. This is the source from which the seer obtains his vision—the prophet his foresight. Many have concentrated themselves up on high ideals in their work, and have received rare knowledge from this source, which they have attributed to beings from another world—from angels, from spirits, from God himself—but all came from within—it was their Higher Self speaking to them. This does not mean that man never receives communications from the other sources just named—far from this, for we know that the latter is often evidenced and experienced. But we do mean that man receives far more messages from the Higher Self than he does from the other sources, and that man is prone to mistake the one for the other. We cannot discuss this matter at length, in this place, for it is foreign to the subject which we are handling at the present time.

Man, by the development of his Spiritual consciousness, may bring himself into a high relationship and contact with this higher part of his nature, and may thus become possessed of knowledge beyond the power of the Intellect to furnish. Certain high powers are also open to a man in this way, but he must beware against using them for any purpose other than the good of his fellow-men, for such prostitution of spiritual powers brings a terrible result in its train. Such is the Law.

And, while it is true that the fullest degree of Spiritual Healing is not open to the average person, still it is likewise true that the healer who is possessed of a degree of Spiritual unfoldment may avail himself of a certain degree of Spiritual power in treating his fellow-men. In fact, the best healers, consciously or unconsciously, make use of this force in this way. And they are right in so doing—it is a proper use of the power. Spiritual Healing may be used in connection with the other forms of healing described and explained in this book, to good advantage, and without interfering with the other treatments. In fact, all conscientious healers should endeavor to give the patients the benefit of this form of treatment in connection with the regular treatments. The Spiritual always working for Good, cannot be misapplied or prostituted in cases of relief to suffering humanity, so the healer need never fear that in so acting he is dragging down the Spiritual to the material level. For the Spiritual permeates everything, and if it may be used to "bring up" those on a lower plane, it is well used.

In the next chapter we shall endeavor to give the student a few explanations and some information regarding the practice of Spiritual Healing, although, as will readily be seen, it is almost impossible to tell one how to do something, that consists in *letting* rather than doing. And we must ask the student to approach this part of the subject with a feeling of sufficient respect, for in Spiritual Healing, one is calling into operation Forces and Power of an entirely different order from those with which man is acquainted in this everyday life. The

Spiritual Healer is allowing himself to be used as a channel for the transmission of that force from the great Ocean of Spirit to the Spiritual Mind of the patient, and he should endeavor to make himself a worthy instrument of that Power and Spirit.

CHAPTER XX

PRACTICE OF SPIRITUAL HEALING

The Spiritual Healer should approach his treatments with respect and appreciation of the mighty Power which he desires to have flow through him for the aid and relief of the patient. He should first quiet his body and mind, and so far as possible relieve his nerves and muscles from strain and contraction, and free his mind from worries and cares and thoughts of the material life. He should endeavor to bring to himself that condition of peaceful, quiet, calm that belongs by right to him or her who realizes the meaning of the terms "Spiritual Mind" and "Spirit." He should endeavor to pass into that mental state in which he feels the nearness of the Ocean of Spirit, of which his Real Self is a drop. He should endeavor to feel "In Tune with the Infinite."

We cannot very well describe in words just what

this condition is like. It must be felt to be understood. But we feel that those who are attracted to this book—or who have attracted it to themselves—will have sufficient realization of what we mean, to enable them to cultivate it still further.

The healer may either place his hands on the patient or otherwise, just as he sees fit. Some Spiritual Healers do not touch the patient, while others feel, instinctively, that they should do so. Be governed by your own intuition in this matter. There seems to be a certain something about the touch of a person through whom the Spirit is flowing, that carries with it a certain indefinable healing power. Remember that Jesus and his apostles healed by Spiritual Power, usually through the "laying on of the hands." So do not hesitate to place your hands on the patient, if you feel moved to do so. In giving the treatment, cast off all responsibility or feeling that *You* are giving the treatment, and keep the idea constantly before you that you are but the channel for the inflow of the Spirit Power. The moment you begin to think that *You* are doing the work, just that moment do you begin to obstruct the source of the Power, and to shut it off. Many good Spiritual Healers have destroyed the efficiency of their work in this way, and by their growing egotism and sense of self-importance have lost entirely the great power that they have had in the beginning, before they were spoiled by success and plaudits of the crowd.

"We have known several striking instances of this in our own experience, and the readers may know of other cases which they will now understand more fully. Beware of this fatal error in Spiritual Healing. *You* do not heal—but Spirit does. Remember this always.

The best way to make yourself a proper channel for the inflow of the Spiritual Healing Power, is to fix in the mind the thought that you are a "channel" through which the healing power flows, and endeavor to mentally "see" or "feel" the inflow and outpouring of Spirit during the entire treatment. The treatment should not last very long—the intuition of the Healer being the best guide. Very often, after practicing this form of healing for a time, such proficiency is acquired that both the healer and the patient can actually "feel" the inflow of Spirit during the treatment. In such cases rest assured that the best conditions have been acquired or found.

Both the healer and the patient should be in the proper state of mind during Spiritual, treatment, for in this way the minds of both are rendered proper instruments or channels for the inflow of Spirit. To acquire this mutual mental condition, it is well for the healer to read to the patient a few lines or paragraphs from some writer on spiritual subjects — being sure to select some writing harmonious to the patient. By this means the minds of both healer and

163

patient are cleared of the more material thoughts, and placed in the best conditions for the treatment.

In these treatments it is not necessary or desirable for the healer to "hold the thought" of the particular form of cure as in the case of Mental Healing. Spirit permeates the organism of the patient, through his or her Spiritual Mind, and tends to render it "whole" or "perfect" all over, without reference to parts or organs. The patient is bathed in a flow of Spirit, and every cell-mind recognizes its presence and is stimulated thereby.

This is all that we can say to you regarding Spiritual treatments. The rest you will discover as you progress in the work. Do not be afraid to try this form of treatment—provided you do it in the right spirit. And you will find that you will become a greater and greater instrument for the expression of the Spirit Healing Power, as time goes on, and your work will grow better and better.

To those who prefer the other forms of treatment mentioned in this book, or who find it advisable to follow the other forms, because of the desires or conditions of their patient, we suggest that they give at least a moment or two of Spiritual treatment, at the close of the other treatment. The patient may, or may not, be told of this—just as the healer thinks best. There is no trace of deception here, for Spirit belongs to all—and all is subservient to Spirit—so that if the healer thinks it well to make use of its Power, without telling the patient, he is justified in doing so. Some patients may be prejudiced against anything bearing the name "Spiritual" because they associate it with "disembodied spirits", "spiritualism", etc., etc. So it would be folly to use the word "spiritual" in talking to these persons. And others may think that anything "spiritual" savors of "religious" things, and that therefore Spiritual Healing might be something contrary to their religious beliefs, etc. Of course, both of these ideas are based on misapprehension, and it would be useless to attempt to explain the matter to such people. And in these cases the better way to give the other treatments, using the terms of that particular treatment, and then give the patient the advantage of the Spiritual treatment as well, without saying anything about it. The patient's ignorance should not prevent him from receiving the best that the healer can give him. In this advise, of course, we do not hold that deception should be used, or untruth indulged in, but merely wish to remind the healer that it is useless and foolish to arouse antagonism by the ill-advised use of names and terms which happen to be misunderstood, or but half understood by certain patients, whose prejudices and bigotry might interfere with the good that you wish to do them.

CHAPTER XXI

CONCLUDING ADVICE

Now that we have acquainted the reader with the theory and practice of the various forms of Psychic Healing, we wish to say a few words to him regarding the practice of the healing power that has been described.

In the first place, do not make the mistake of becoming bigoted, and narrow in your views of healing. Do not follow the example of so many of the practitioners of drug healing, and revile and abuse those who may differ from you. Be broad – be generous – be liberal. Give each man the same liberty of opinion that you demand for yourself. Do not force your views on others, but always be willing to answer a courteous and earnest inquiry for information.

Do not start in to abuse the drug practitioners. This

is not right from any point of view, and as a mere matter of policy is unwise. Make your own work so good that people will seek you on that account, and do not try to build up a practice on the abuse of others. There are many drug practitioners who are splendid men, and who, at the bottom of their hearts are in full sympathy with the finer forms of healing but who are not able to express themselves fully, owing to popular prejudice and the fear of getting into trouble with the medical boards. Such men give drugs because they have to do so, and at the same time manage to "work in" psychic healing without the knowledge of the patient, which fact accounts for the success of many a quiet physician. As for those abusive members of the medical fraternity, who go about reviling the mental or spiritual healer— why, just let them alone. They will reap their own harvest of hate and abuse, and so do not I commit the folly of entering into their whirlpool. Practice "passive resistance" toward them, and you will find it far more efficacious than the "active resistance" of the world about you. This is a truth known to all students of occultism, and is one of the most "practical" 'bits of advice known to man.

Do not neglect the attention to the natural laws of the body, as mentioned in an early chapter. See that the patient acts in accord with these natural laws of his being, and you will be thereby enabled to get much better results, in a much, shorter time. Proper nutrition, and proper elimination must be had before any system of healing is effective. And no matter if the patient were cured instantaneously by the most powerful form of psychic healing, still, if he were to continue to neglect the primary physical laws of his being he would sooner or later get back to his old diseased condition. This is a fact that many psychic healers ignore or refuse to accept, but rest assured that it is absolute truth, and that it will be found to be fully operative at all times, and in all cases. Common sense will show the correctness of this view of the matter. Don't be like an ostrich, and hide your head so that you will not see the truth regarding the physical laws. Do not let metaphysics make you refuse to recognize physics. This is as absurd a position as is that of the physician who refuses to see the great truths of metaphysics.

Be full of the spirit of Love and Kindness for your patients, but do not allow a false sympathy to cause you to take on their conditions, or to let them drain your vitality from you. Refuse to allow this, and do not let yourself become "passive" to the patient, or to exhibit a "negative" condition to him. Keep "positive" and "active" in your relations to him, else you may discover the effects of the "vampirism" of some sick people, who like nothing better than to drain the vitality of the healer, that they may be benefited or strengthened. Give them the benefit of your knowledge and skill, but do not allow them to absorb your life and vitality—for that does not belong to them. So, therefore, do not "let go" of yourself in the direction of "feeling" their condition too strongly—beware of a certain kind of Sympathy—or rather, of something miscalled Sympathy.

The nearer you are in consciousness to the Source of all Power, the greater will be your healing power. Remember always that back of all the Power of the Universe is that Infinite Power, which is the source of all Power and Energy. Remember that you are as a particle of this one Infinite Life, and that all that is Real about you is so because of your relationship with that Infinite Being. Try to realize this fully, and you will find that with the recognition will come a strength and power far surpassing anything that you have before known, or acquired by any other means. This is the source of all real power, and it is open to him or her who seeks it.

The following Affirmation or Mantram may be found useful, if repeated before giving a treatment:

AFFIRMATION OF MANTRAM

Oh, thou Great Infinite Power Thou Great Flame of Life, of which I am but a spark I open myself to thy Healing Power, that it may flow through me to strengthen, build-

up, and make whole, this brother (or sister) in Life. Let thy Power flow through me to the end that he (or she) may receive thy vivifying Energy and Strength and Life, and be able to manifest the same as Health, Strength, and Vigor. Make me a worthy channel for thy Power, and use me for Good.

Peace be with thee, in thy Healing Work.

Printed in Great Britain
by Amazon